HONEY
AND
GEMMA

HONEY AND GEMMA

Peter Dobson

Futura

A *Futura* Book

Copyright © Peter Dobson 1984

This edition published in 1985
by Futura Publications, a Division of
Macdonald & Co (Publishers) Ltd
London & Sydney

ISBN 0 7088 2621 0

Printed and bound in Great Britain by
Collins, Glasgow

Futura Publications
A Division of
Macdonald & Co (Publishers) Ltd
Maxwell House
74 Worship Street
London EC2A 2EN

A BPCC plc Company

Contents

CHAPTER 1

False Starts and Early Days

Looking back now I can see it was folly for a middle-aged man, set in his self-indulgent ways, to get involved with dogs at all, particularly when his wife and children were terrified of them. Jane was frightened of dogs for the sufficient reason that her parents had kept a blood-stained and white Springer Spaniel with halitosis, that bit first and asked questions afterwards, and she had transmitted her terror to the children. The urge to own a dog, however, is as powerful an emotion as falling in love, and whilst I can't recall a case of anyone trotting happily down the aisle with a Golden Retriever on his arm, I do think it would be a good thing to have to go through some sort of solemn service to become a dog owner. The marriage service would do very nicely, leaving out the naughty bits of course, but coming on strong with, 'Do you take this Wolfhound to be your lawfully wedded pet, to exercise and feed from this day forward, to love, honour and obey all doggy whims until death do you part?' Then you slip a collar on its neck, wait for permission to give it a big kiss, fork out your licence money in the vestry, and there you are; pronounced man and dog. A bit one-sided maybe, but no true dog lover is going to mind that.

It was the family fear that kept dogs at bay, and the only one we had in ages was a mythical beast named

Bonzo which was said to live in our youngest daughter's voluminous nappies. Young Samantha could have talked a horse-race commentator into breathless collapse by the time she was six months old, but was a late developer on potty training and paranoiac about dogs, and Bonzo was invented to make a joke instead of an issue out of it. Samantha enjoyed the joke for a few weeks until the day when she was having a nervous breakdown over a long-haired Dachshund puppy that was doing its Hound of the Baskerville's impressions three quarters of a mile away.

'Never mind about him, luvvy,' I comforted. 'How's young Bonzo getting on?' 'I done a wee wee on him,' she snapped and that was the end of dog ownership for some years. I was sorry to see him go.

After that we had a succession of animals to try and assuage the dog-lust but none of them succeeded. The first arrival was Willie, a black and white round-headed kitten that a friend discovered one snowy morning tied up in a sack on an underground station. The friend was soft-hearted but not soft-headed, and he rescued the kitten and rang up to ask if the kids would like it. I told him that they'd hate it, but he brought it round all the same, along with a bottle of cheap red wine, most of which he drank himself. So of course we became cat owners. It wouldn't have been so bad if Willie had been a normal, free-loading, affectionate pussy cat, but being tied up in a sack had understandably soured his nature and whilst he was a great character, like most great characters he had a very nasty streak. He decimated the bird and rodent population for several gardens around, and at the time of year that baby birds were being thrown off high buildings by their parents to 'go solo' for the first time I spent hours mounting crash guard on the feathered wrecks whilst further instructions were shrieked at them from the tree tops.

As the children grew up, there came a succession of gerbils and hamsters. All that you can really say for hamsters is that they can get an awful lot of hamster food into their mouths at one time, but they were quite sweet, I suppose, and visiting drunkards loved them. We let them out one evening after a dinner party – for no good reason that I can remember except that it seemed like a good idea at the time – and they crawled through a small hole in the back of the settee and disappeared into the bowels of the thing, followed by several apparently respectable guests, maddened by vin rosé. By the time the hamsters and guests were recovered, and the hamsters comforted and tucked up in bed we badly needed a new settee and the place was littered with string, springs, straw, stuffing, and hamster droppings.

Gerbils are much the same as far as I'm concerned, although we kept them from 'pot-holing' in the furniture and the first pair that we had were amputees, one having a left arm only, and the other a right. Willie, the cat, got Lefty, which caused a fair old family Strindberg, and got the casual gardener at the same time as the man courageously tried to rescue Lefty. Willie laid his arm open from wrist to elbow and it cost me a fiver to stop him airing his opinion of cats in front of the children.

We got a new companion for Righty from the local pet shop and Righty fought with it, so we took it back to the shop, as soon as we could take its bandages off, and explained our problem to the lady who ran the place. This rather unsympathetic person, whom I had always suspected of war crimes, had a simple solution redolent of enlightened self-interest. 'Give zer udder vun to zer cat' she rasped, 'und buy two new vuns.'

When Samantha was eight she came home from school with a moving story of a rabbit condemned to pie-filling if not collected from the RSPCA before tomorrow's dawn. Jane and I presented a united front on this one and the bones of our reply, when stripped of diplomatic phrases, was 'Tough'. As both our children had been brought up according to Spock, there were heel-drumming tantrums, tears, and accusations of heartlessness, which is how Wabbit came to join the household. Wabbit was large, black and phlegmatic, and Willie was terrified of him, which shows that he knew something.

I had always thought of rabbits as being harmless but apparently they are not. We met an American lady at the vet's one morning who was greatly impressed that Wabbit was sitting on my knee.

'Boy,' she said. 'Are you ever brave. I wouldn't go near our Goddamn rabbit. He took two of my daughter's fingers nearly off, yesterday. And he chases our Alsatian.'

Wabbit mucked up our image with our neighbours. Our new neighbours that is; it was a funny thing but whatever district we moved to in London shortly afterwards underwent a process vilely and inaccurately known as 'gentrification,' and all our nice, shambling, boozy, cultured neighbours moved away, selling their run-down houses to over-hygienic acquisitive whizz kids and their stainless steel wives, who immediately installed sauna baths and bidets. Two newcomers who were converting a house up the road from a home into a space station called round to patronize us one Sunday morning and were only politely appalled at our dereliction until they saw Wabbit, who had the hop of the house, sitting quietly in a corner of the kitchen engaged in current affairs. They never called again, and never asked us to baby-sit for their horribly clever, whey-faced children.

Having all these creatures lounging about the house eating their heads off prepared Jane and the children for dog-owning, which in the end sort of snuck up on us. We got off to what turned out fortunately to be a false start when we nearly became the full-time providers for a mountainous Pyrenean dog named Hector which I met at a surrealist painter's house one evening. Gordon, the painter, was a dour Glaswegian. When he opened his front door to me with his customary scowl of welcome, there was Hector's huge face peering at me over the top of his head. In the half light of the hall an unexpected Hector was an unnerving experience and my first thought was that a dissident Yeti had taken Gordon hostage. I was on my way to get the SAS when Gordon called me back.

'For Goad's sake come away in, son,' he said disgustedly. 'It's only a dawg.'

Hector and I were instant chums. It turned out that he belonged to a vet and his vet wife, who were looking for a good home for him as they were off to Africa for some unspecified purpose, which I now suspect was to escape from Hector and his appetite. I went home with delusions of grandeur and persuaded the family that we should have him as Hector protector of the home and garden, and lovable ladies' companion and pet. I forgot to mention that the great lump, who wasn't yet fully grown, weighed fourteen stone, stood seven foot three in his socks and scoffed a baby's bathful of meat and assorted vegetables every day and a half-hundred-weight sack of biscuits every week.

Mr and Mrs Vet lived in Melton Mowbray and I arranged that we should spend the day with them for the family to give Hector the glad eye. When we rolled up Hector was leaning over a six foot fence waiting to greet us. 'Jesus,' said Samantha, a well-spoken child who went to a church school. 'My God,' said Jane. 'Where do they get the Christians to feed it?' Our eldest daughter Jacky said nothing at all, but began to cry. Laughing merrily at their little joke I bullied them out of the car but they shot back in again screaming when Hector began galumphing about, bellowing deep ambiguous woofs at them. They sat huddled together sobbing, absolutely refusing to come out to be mauled and eaten, whilst I comforted and pleaded, and Hector raged up and down battering the fence. In the end I flew into a huff and drove brooding back to London. Secretly, though, I wasn't heartbroken as even I had begun to realize that Hector could well turn out to be a double-decker, milkman-eating, incubus.

This debacle, or should I say dog bark, had its uses, for when Felicity, a fearfully grand friend of Jane's, found a more normal-sized animal for us they accepted it gratefully.

Felicity's life is arranged for the pleasure and convenience of a strong-minded miniature Dachshund bitch named Hermione who is probably a reincarnation of Queen Victoria. While on a short royal tour of the smarter part of town one evening, they came across Honey, a Labrador pup who, although she was tiny, was much bigger than Hermione. A large and coarse-natured Labrador with a cold wet nose had done something very personal to Hermione some years before, and this lese-majesty had left her biased against the breed, so when Felicity scooped the puppy off the pavement and babbled baby talk to it she was not amused and screamed with rage and indignation. Felicity dealt the regal ribs a sharp tap with the toe of an expensive suede boot and went on crooning over the wriggling puppy until she eventually noticed a tall and diffident young man on the other end of the lead who was beginning to wonder if he was invisible. After a few minutes in Felicity's company he probably wished that he was, as she sternly interrogated him concerning the puppy's pedigree, Epivax, age, name and gender; and his own particulars, pedigree, prospects and qualifications for dog ownership.

'Extraordinary chap,' said Felicity. 'He told me about his vasectomy.' Having wrung the last drop of information from the poor lad and sent him on his way Felicity sped round to us in a severely besotted state of mind and to cut a long story short her message was simple: young Honey needed a new home, and we were it. It seemed the young man had given Honey to his wife as a birthday present, never pausing to think that as they had three small children, another on the way, two kittens and a guinea pig, and lived on the fifth floor of a block of flats with unusually high ceilings and no lift, a subscription to the nappy service might have been a better choice.

Next morning I scaled the ten flights of marble stairs up to their flat to find out if all that Felicity had said about Honey was true, which it was. In fact, a lot of what she had said had been an understatement. Honey looked just like a Seal pup trying to wag itself to pieces. I took her home and gave her to Jane who was in the bath, which turned out to be a good place for her to

13

forget she was frightened of dogs, and for a Labrador puppy to acquire a taste for bathwater.

Becoming proud dog-owners changed our lives completely and for the better. My usual morning tasks were to wake the children in time to be late for school, distribute hot drinks all round, and then to spend some time in the bathroom disguising the signs of encroaching senility. To these was now added dog-walking in the park, which was at the end of the road, for at least half an hour. It was at this stage of my development as a dog-owner that I had a motor-cycle accident that put me out of the running, and walking, for a couple of weeks, but I so enjoyed the morning walks that as soon as I'd recovered enough to put one crutch before the other I was out in the park again with the bottom of my plaster wrapped in a green plastic bag. For at least two minutes I received more attention from the other dog-walkers than did Honey. She, being intensely feminine, took advantage of my disability and behaved badly. She had a lovely time one morning playing on both sides of a posh school football match, which she and the boys greatly enjoyed, but their master, who took such things seriously, did not. The two of us charged muddily along in pursuit, encouraged from the sidelines by schoolboy jokes about athlete's crutch, with 'sir' hoping I'd break the other leg. One can get along quite fast on crutches, until one falls over, and between us we eventually drove her from the field. Then she refused to come home, and ran away laughing every time I got close. In the end I was so tired and angry that I threw a crutch at her, which she picked up and ran off with. I caught up with her at the front gate, by which time I was perspiring and in an ugly mood. However, it is difficult to beat a dog satisfactorily whilst standing exhausted on one leg, and she looked so charming standing there with her brow all wrinkled trying to solve the tremendous problem of getting a wide crutch through a narrow gap, that her punishment was a ten-minute lesson in how to achieve the task – a complete waste of time, as she never did grasp the principle.

Her first, and only, season was an interesting experience for us all. For a start, she was 'got at' by something shaggy and unsuitable, which had swarmed over the garden fence, and she had to be taken to the vet and expensively injected. A crowd of dogs lay about the front garden throughout, over-watering the azalias and rotting the gateposts. They were, for the most part, amiable and frightfully well mannered. The only exception was a daft and woolly animal that looked rather like an unmade Bedlington and which came over all unnecessary whenever any of us left the shelter of the house. After a few steps it had formed a romantic attachment to one's leg and I soon tired of its unrequited love and took it to the police, driving with one hand and fending off its advances with the other. It could have been rather flattering, I suppose, if I hadn't known it was so promiscuous. It greeted the desk sergeant like an old friend, with no hint of concupiscence, and when I brought charges of gross indecency, child molestation and attempted adultery against it he only laughed. I was the third person that month to bring it in. He gave me the owner's address and asked me to return it. 'See if you can find out what they feed it on?' he said thoughtfully. I took it home and was rude to its owner but next day it was back on station.

After that we had Honey spayed, and don't let anyone tell you that spaying makes bitches fat. What causes obesity in bitches is the same thing that causes obesity in the rest of us; too much food and too little exercise. We reluctantly left Honey with Fred the vet and went back in the afternoon to collect her. Still drowsy from the anaesthetic she tottered down the path towards us, face all wrinkled up with smiles and rear end wagging.

Even after she was spayed she continued to attract gentleman animals, none of whose attentions struck me as being the least bit honourable. Not that one could blame them; there was just something about her. She even corrupted our rabbit. Wabbit had lived a contemplative life hopping about the house, but when Honey arrived he hopped about after her with a funny look in his eye. His beastlier rabbity instincts overwhelmed his nobler emotions the day that Curruthers collapsed on our door step in a distressed condition asking to be put in touch with our doctor.

Curruthers is one of our many eccentric motor-cycling friends, more eccentric than most. Scion and heavy-duty black sheep of an aristocratic family, there he suddenly was, all tweeds and eyebrows, in the last agonizing stages of a heart attack. So he said. Honey made nursing noises at him and sank down at his feet by the kitchen table while we applied hot sweet tea and crumpets and listened sympathetically. His death throes didn't seem to have affected his appetite much, or his powers of speech, but he reckoned he was slipping away nevertheless.

What arrested his decline was the rabbit. It didn't actually kick the door open but it did make a pretty forceful entrance. Curruthers looked cross. Nobody likes to have his death scene upstaged by a rabbit barging into it. As for Wabbit, he was no longer the lethargic creature we had known and fallen over. He had obviously come to a crossroads in his life and had made

'Honey made nursing noises . . .'

a decision. It must be an uncommon occurrence to have a dying man munching crumpets in your kitchen while a large black rabbit bursts in upon an urgent errand, and we rather forgot about Curruther's little trouble, and even Curruthers was riveted, put out as he was. Wabbit came straight to the point, and hopping round behind young Honey who was nervously watching him over her shoulder, thumped his hind legs on the floor, spat on his paws and leapt boldly aboard. No flowers, no chocolates, no 'shall I compare thee to a summer's day.'

If we were surprised, Honey was horrified; she might have her little ways but miscegenation wasn't one of them. She goggled at him for a moment and then there was uproar. Over the cries of a well-bitten rabbit departing at speed came the snarls of an outraged maiden scrabbling for grip on a slippery floor and bringing a fresh new meaning to 'coitus interruptus' as she left in furious pursuit. When the tumult died away we turned to Curruthers, who seemed much improved. Apparently it didn't hurt, even when he laughed, which was just as well as he was holding his sides whilst the tears ran down his distinguished features. He never mentioned his heart attack again.

Honey was such a success with man, woman and gentleman beast that several people we knew went out and bought Labrador puppies on the strength of her charms. I wouldn't claim that we introduced the Labrador to London but we certainly helped to popularize the species. One of these puppies was Gemma, who waddled in to the park one morning all fat and jolly and a fully paid-up member of Epivax. Bigger built than Honey and a rich brown colour, she looked more like a dog than a bitch. The poor dear was a bit of a disappointment to her new parents who weren't really doggy at all and more interested in keeping up with the Cohens than pandering to the whims of a high-spirited puppy. Their eldest daughter, however, adored young Gemma and took her for long walks, morning and evening: she and Honey became great friends.

Every morning brought fresh tales of the depredations of Gemma, all variations on a familiar theme of chewings, thievings and abscondings to rummage the neighbourhood dustbins, returning fat, filthy and happily apologetic four or five hours later. After a year of roaming the streets with murder in their hearts cooing the wanderer's name in vain, of cleaning the slightly digested remnants of new brocade curtains off new carpets after Gemma's usually heroic stomach had fallen down on the job, of trudging back to the butcher to replace what young Gemma had laid tooth to, of wasting valuable house shampooing time getting dog's hair off their sheepskin coats, her owners decided they were not dog-lovers. Dog-owning was not them.

The little girl's mother told Jane that Gemma was going to be a guide dog. Jane, out of common decency, said that she thought that the blind already had enough to contend with and we would buy her instead. So there we were: a two dog family. Or to be more specific a two child, two parent, two dog, two car, two motorbike, one cat and one rabbit family. And if that sounds like ostentation let me say that one of the cars was a Triumph Herald convertible that the neighbours, who were mostly Socialist Stockbrokers, considered was mucking up the district.

The motorbikes I hardly used. We had quickly got into a state of mind, although not to the point of total idiocy, such that if we couldn't take the dogs we didn't

want to go. Also I was a little disillusioned with the
motorbikes by the accident I mentioned in which I was
knocked off a beautiful new bike by a lady who did a
sudden U-turn – in a car, of course – just as I was
passing. She said in court that she hadn't seen me,
which was certainly true as she hadn't looked. I lay in
the road for a while, with a badly broken leg, attended
by two passing doctors and a charming Roman Catholic
priest. It was really quite a pleasant social occasion, after
I had got over the notion that my leg was severed inside
the boot. I was carried off, protesting, to what was
probably the worst hospital in London, which meant
they were working at it. They rang up Jane and told her
that I had been in a bad road accident, although they
knew quite well that I had only broken a tib. and a fib.
The point of this dogged recitation of injury and
suffering is that when the shock of this cruelly thoughtless announcement caught up with Jane in the depres-
sive small hours, a sleepy puppy was roused from its
bed and carried up to ours to provide comforts and
cuddles until I could resume my duties. Whether or not
Jane really intended young Honey to remain on the bed
rather than in it, I don't know, but when I finally
dragged several stone of thigh-to-toe plaster upstairs,
for the first time in weeks, I had the distinct impression
that it was Honey's bed I was climbing into, and
wouldn't I be more comfortable in my basket in the
kitchen.

When Gemma came along we were faced with a moral
dilemma, as we could hardly take Honey up to bed with
us and leave Gemma downstairs, especially as she was
slightly disturbed about changing homes. When she
came to us she was pretty well trained: she might eat
the furniture but she never sat on it. When she first saw

Honey sprawling on the settee whilst I sat on the floor she goggled a bit. But she soon got into the swing of things and was quickly snuggled up in bed with the rest of us with little or no crisis of conscience. Honey wasn't in the least jealous. She was fond of Gemma and delighted that we were a two dog family. All we needed was another comfortable chair and a bigger bed.

My parents were not delighted. The old man's first reaction when he heard about Gemma was to say, 'Oh God. I hope this one keeps its tail down.' Their second, joint, reaction was fury at our profligacy in doubling our dog-food and vet's bills. They were so cross about Gemma that they didn't speak to us for months.

In the June before we became a two dog family Honey had a nasty swimming accident in the Isle of Man. I had taken the family over for the TT Races. Or to be truthful, I had gone for the races, and the social whirl, and the family were there to enjoy the island, which is really very beautiful – they scampered for home before the races actually started and my motorcycling friends turned up.

Being a tax haven the Isle of Man is full of white people from Black Africa called by the Manx 'When I's', and they get along quite nicely with the natives once they stop addressing them as 'boy' and expecting to be called 'bwana' in return. Due to the habits of a lifetime, and to help them forget what a ghastly climate they are living in, the 'When I's' drink rather a lot. On the day Honey hurt herself we had been to lunch with some Rhodesian friends at Union Mills who also drank rather a lot, and after a splendid lunch we tottered out for a walk to exhale some of the fumes. We were reeling about giggling in the valley of the River Dhoo when Honey jumped in for a swim. Standing up through a submerged plank was a sharp and rusty spike and the poor love jumped right onto it, impaling her nearside rear paw.

I got wet and bloody, and very sober, getting her off the spike and carrying her back to the house. She was very brave. She made a fuss when it happened but nothing like the fuss I'd have made had it happened to me; after that she lay down and looked noble. We carried out what first aid we could, stopped the bleeding and got her to a vet as fast as possible. She had a bad wound but hadn't damaged anything vital, and he said he'd prefer not to bandage it up, but we must bathe it in warm salty water in the morning, and last thing at night. All very well with a wife to play doctors and nurses with but a bit of a struggle on one's own after the family had gone home – I always kept Honey with me as she too enjoyed the social round.

Another thing that made midnight dog-bathing difficult in the Isle of Man was the problem of summoning up enough strength of mind to get to bed sober. This was especially true of our hotel, since to go up to bed one had to pass through a bar frequented by the local vicar and many of his parishioners, who liked to keep me up until the small hours talking fascinating Celtic nonsense. The vicar was worse than the rest of them and drank pints of draught Guinness each containing a large gin, a drink that he called a 'dog's nose'; most of his conversation after a few of these was in Erse, Norse and Swahili which didn't seem to matter a lot as one got into the spirit of the evening.

After a few nights in his company I needed an early night and managing to evade the vicar crept up to bed at around half past twelve in company with my motor-cycling friends who were in the next room. Having said goodnight to them I set about bathing Honey's wound.

Now, show a Labrador a large stretch of cold and filthy water and it will leap into it with happy shouts. Show one a bowl of lukewarm salty water for medicinal purposes, and it goes to pieces immediately and slinks off looking reproachfully over its shoulder. Honey couldn't slink far and was retrieved firmly by the tail, and her foot placed in the water. She gave me a tragic look and took it out again. I replaced it with soothing words, and she lifted it out and stood on three legs with the bad paw in the air, looking suicidal. I explained to her at some length that the treatment was for her own good, not my entertainment, and plonked it back in the brine. She hung her head in dark despair and took it out again. This went on until the water got cold, she got bored, and I spoke to her severely. I then got more warm water, shoved her foot into it, ignored the expression on her face that conveyed quite clearly that she had lost the will to live, and went out to clean my teeth. When I came back she had gone to bed, so I gave up and went to bed too.

Having been up half the night I woke late in the morning, trod in the bowl of healing waters and went down to breakfast in a bad temper, feeling worse in mind and liver than if I'd stayed up drinking with the Reverend and his dissipated congregation. The dining room was crowded with strangers newly arrived off the midnight boat from Liverpool and in the corner my friends stopped slaughtering the toast and went into a well-rehearsed familiar-sounding routine.

'Poor old Honey-bunny,' they chorused cruelly. 'Bring its nasty woundsies over here, then.'

'Whatever . . . Androcles said to the lion . . . would sound pretty
ridiculous.'

'Let's put a treasure's pawsy wawsy in the nice warm water.'

'Stand still, you furry oaf.'

'There, there, isn't that soothing for a piggy's tootsie?'

'Honey. That is a no no and a naughty badness. A puppy won't ever get well unless its daddy dunks its horrid injuries.'

'Stand still you witless mutt, or I'll twist your rotten tail off.'

In spite of this public humiliation I still believe that baby talk has a calming effect on most reasonable animals, and if whatever it was that Androcles said to the lion had been recorded no doubt it would sound pretty ridiculous.

CHAPTER 2

Honey and Gemma

There are many shades of Labrador fur but officially those that are not black, or liver-coloured, are classified as yellow. In fact Honey is nearly white, and Gemma, when we first had her, was a rich brown. Over the years she has faded to be almost Honey's colour, probably from a vain desire to look like a matched pair, and it's now very difficult to tell them apart at a quick glance, except that Honey is pretty and Gemma is noble, if only in appearance.

It would be hard to imagine two bitches of the same breed more different than Honey and Gemma. I don't much like the term 'bitch' applied to them as they are much too nice but there seems to be no way round it. Honey is very much the sort of girl who wears a fur coat and no knickers. She is very attractive to dogs, thoroughly enjoying their advances no matter what sort of dog it is that's paying court. She has a slight preference for gentleman Labradors of all colours, but so long as it's male she is not greatly bothered. Although it isn't mentioned in her pedigree, she obviously springs from a long line of trollops, for every time a suitor appears, which is frequently, she rolls on her back with her legs in the air, a silly smile on her face, which makes it difficult to exercise her properly, since on the average walk she spends more time on her back than she does on her feet and returns home thoroughly rested. My dog-hating father found Honey's shameless flauntings embarrassing, but most people think them funny and rather endearing. I used to tell people that she'd caught the habit from my wife, although I was careful never to make jests of this kind, or of any other kind, in front of her parents. Quite often Honey lies smirking sexily with her eyes tight shut long after the gentleman has lost interest. Occasionally she has the grace to scramble to her feet looking a bit sheepish when this is unkindly pointed out, but she really does not understand what modesty is about.

Gemma, on the other hand, is the sort of girl who wears a fur coat and two pairs of knickers, with her knife, fork and spoon tucked into the elastic. She is much more interested in food than flirting and discourages over-familiarity by sitting down firmly on admirers' noses and pretending it isn't happening until they jerk their faces free and go away. She too had been expensively spayed by Fred the Veterinary before we got her, which I think was just as well, as had she endured the necessary preliminaries to motherhood she might have made a light snack of her puppies.

Their eating habits also differ, for whilst Honey watches the preparation of her dinner with her nose twitching and a polite smile hovering on the lips, Gemma jumps up and down slobbering and yipping. Honey shoves her face into the plat de jour, sniffs it appreciatively, murmurs grace and eats in a civilized manner, thirty-three bites to a mouthful and no feet in the trough. Gemma knocks the dish out of your hand and bolts the chef's special before it hit the mat. She'll never wear her teeth out, as the food just brushes past them to hurtle down her throat, landing in the steaming vaults of her stomach more or less in its original condition. She must have the fastest peristalsis in the West, and Porton Down might be interested to analyse a sample of her digestive juices. She really ought to have a Dangerous Liquid warning pasted on her flanks.

Gemma's motto is 'Snatch and Consume', and feeding her titbits from the table can be a nasty experience if not preceded by a three-minute lecture on dainty manners. She has had many a sharp whack on the nose for nipping fingers but it doesn't make any difference. Honey, by contrast, would not be out of place at a vicarage garden party, crooking her eye-claw whilst slurping her tea and making inroads into the cucumber sandwiches.

The only time that Honey ever barked was at the rabbit. He had been following her about the house with an expression of furtive lust on his face and thoughtlessly peered over the edge of her bowl while she was breakfasting.

It can only have been curiosity as I can't imagine a rabbit scoffing Pedigree Chum, especially as he might have known somebody in it. Honey went berserk and actually barked. It was a fine soprano bark and Maria Callas couldn't have done better; certainly not on all fours with her mouth full of dog food. Such a shrill and sudden sound quite electrified poor Wabbit, who took off like an electric hare pursued by greyhounds. Honey was so appalled that she couldn't eat another thing and immediately sought out every member of the family, excepting Wabbit, and apologized profusely for her outburst.

Gemma is very different. To be honest, she is a bit of a lout. For a start she looks more like a dog than a bitch and goes in for machismo. When the bell rings, off goes

Gemma: all suppressed violence and piercing barks. Honey scampers along with her, but silently. Whoever is at the door is soundly and indiscriminately welcomed. If the Mad Axeman called he'd probably be overwhelmed by doggy mateyness before he could do us a mischief. The proceedings calls for five minutes of ritual uproar. If it is anyone that Honey is particularly fond of, which is almost everybody, she dashes round and round them sneezing with excitement and making a ridiculous mooing sound known as 'the love noise'. Gemma clambers energetically all over them, shouting happily. The visitors bound about trying to defend themselves, and the rest of us bound about shouting and beating at the dogs. Gemma then dashes off and comes back with a present in her mouth: a velvet cushion; an expensive shoe; or a tea towel. All our tea towels are in rags where Gemma has hauled them off their hooks. The greeting is then rounded off with a running fight spilling over into the sitting room, where chairs are knocked over and drinks swept from occasional tables before order can be restored with blows and curses and the dogs remember how tired they were before the doorbell rang and fall down snoring on the visitors' feet. If the visitor is well dressed and doesn't much like dogs he really gets the adhesive dog's-hair-and-slobber treatment from Honey, who tries to climb on his lap for a bit of a rest, and there is more excitement as she is dragged off with apologies. By this time the whole house absolutely reeks of dogs. Well-dressed people who don't much like dogs rarely call again.

Another of the many differences in the dogs' personalities is their attitude to the vet. Honey is terrified and blubs all the way to the surgery, although she loves him dearly. Gemma doesn't care, although she would rather go to a good restaurant, but lives in hope of finding something to eat under the chairs in the waiting room. Fred, our vet, is able and amiable and nothing to be frightened of, has done his share of bullock wrestling, mostly on the winning side, weighs something over two hundredweight and makes John Bull look faintly anaemic. Fred is very fond of dogs but not of Welshmen, having been bitten by one once during a game of rugby and claims to be the president of the 'Rebuild Offa's Dyke Society'. Our daughter Samantha once rescued the wreckage of a mongrel puppy from Battersea and took it straight round to him, at my expense, for mouth to mouth resuscitation. Fred cradled it in his huge arms, with a very soppy look on his huge red face. 'Poor little scrap,' he crooned. 'Needs lots of love and cuddles.' Under Fred's care and direction the pup has grown up to be large and vigorous, and the fact that it is absolutely daft and looks like a pterodactyl/Old English Sheepdog cross is hardly Fred's fault.

At one time we were at the surgery so frequently that I asked Fred if he'd sell me a season ticket. Willie the cat was always getting into fights and losing, which wasn't really surprising as the cats that he chose to fight with were more like bears. At least, I imagine he lost, considering his wounds. Had he won I would have spent a lot of time in the garden burying dead cats. The place would have been like the American Cemetery. After all, one could hardly keep appearing on the neighbours' doorsteps with the disembowelled remnants of their late pets on a tea tray and saying such things as 'I found Fluffy in the Ha Ha, I don't think he's very well'. Fred, whilst not so fond of cats, was very good with them. He was sewing Willie's head back on one day when Willie went for him. 'Keep your claws to yourself, Willie,' said Fred pleasantly, and Willie never gave him any more trouble.

The dogs got a lot of heartless fun out of Willie's fights. His greatest foe was a terrible neckless tom called Thugcat. I used to keep a fatherly eye on their combats to make sure they were conducted under Queensberry rules, and when most of the fur that was flying was obviously flying off our Willie, I would let the dogs out to break up the clinch. Being sporting dogs they were commendably impartial and used to see Thugcat off the premises first and then come back to chase Willie.

Thugcat's career of violence came to a nasty end one day when he called at the house while the dogs were out on business. After Kung Fu-ing Willie into a stretcher case in the first round, he swaggered off chewing on our champion's name and address disc, only to run into the world's largest cat which was obviously lying in wait for him. I didn't care for Thugcat, but the sound-effects were enough to make one purse the lips and wince, especially when the assailant awarded himself the ears and the tail. A few weeks in intensive care probably gave Thugcat time to reflect upon his way of life and when he returned to the district he was a different animal, quite apart from lacking both ears and a tail. He had about him a sort of air of saintly gentility which even Willie and the dogs respected.

Probably the only other outstanding difference between the dogs shows up on country walks which, as we moved to the country last year, are the sort of walks we mostly take. The dogs enjoy the country and so do we, my only reservation about it being that it seems to be infested with professed Christians whom I previously thought of only as lion food and generally managed to avoid, thinking of them as rather unhealthy. Enforced contact has not caused me to modify my opinion and if I need spiritual comfort I shall go to the pub. The only snag about our pub is that they won't have dogs in the saloon bar, and whilst I prefer public bar people, I dislike public bar discomfort, which only goes to show how difficult life really is.

On the afore-mentioned walks, Gemma likes to carry huge sticks. She quarters the ground looking for one, her tail rotating in proper Labrador fashion, and when she's found one she carries it for miles, walking to heel with her head held high and her tail swinging, looking idiotically pleased with herself.

While Gemma is gathering winter fuel Honey is hunting, her nose to the ground in full sniff, rather like Gogool at a witch hunt in 'King Solomon's Mines'. She rarely uses her eyes when hunting and sniggering wildlife is forever leaping out of the boskage without her noticing, well on its way home before she discovers where it used to be two seconds before. We once watched her going nearly out of her mind with excitement on one side of a very slender willow sapling on a river bank, while leaning against the other side a succulent water rat was doing his whiskers and whistling through his teeth. When Honey finally worked out where the delicious smell was coming from she shot round the tree, all teeth and eyes, just in time to see the tip of his tail disappearing down a hole in the opposite bank.

If she does catch sight of any small or medium-sized furry that doesn't look very fierce it is furiously pursued, although she pretends not to see anything larger than a hare, and a herd of deer she once came across in the Ashridge Forest was totally ignored.

'. . . they preferred not to believe in elephants . . .'

H.A.G.-B

Both dogs are life-long sufferers from Lack of Moral Fibre, although I don't think that was the trouble the day that we walked them across Regent's Park to show them the elephants in the zoo. I think they preferred not to believe in elephants, which was difficult as the wind was carrying a pungently pachydermic pong and we were doing our best to make them notice as we wanted to see what they thought. 'Shufti the lovely big jumbos, darlings.' Not a flicker. Nothing. Gemma even pretended to think that the smell of elephant was somebody's lunch cooking. In fairness to Gemma it is possible that she didn't see them, as her eyesight is terrible. She couldn't see a car at twenty-five yards, never mind a number plate, or even a Yorkshire Pudding at twenty-five feet, highly motivated as she is. She only occasionally joins in one of Honey's hunts, and then without really knowing what is going on, but there is always the hope that Honey might be off to a free distribution of veal-and-ham pie, or has discovered a party of Distressed Gentlefolk feebly picnicking.

The nice thing about the hunts that Honey organizes is their harmlessness. To see the pair of them chasing hares is marvellous, as they, and the hares, all enjoy the exercise. It gives the hares a bit of a laugh, and the only danger to either party is a sprained ankle. Honey did once catch a sobbing baby rabbit that had mistimed its departure and fallen over its ears, and she was most sympathetic, and licked it better, and saw it home to its mum.

Now that I think about it they very nearly did catch a hare once, or at least were in with a chance, when one came loping up the road towards us early, which is about 9.30, one morning. Significantly it was in March and in the Isle of Man where the population is eccentric enough all the year round and heaven knows what the hares are like. I told the dogs it was a friend and they sat down and watched in disbelief as he hopped along towards us, all unconcerned, until he was so close that even Gemma could see him. Then he sat down for a bit of a think. Somewhere, not too far away no doubt, a lady hare was watching him, all starry-eyed, or thinking what a berk he was, and if hare's habits are anything like rabbit's habits I imagine that she was what he was thinking about. Nobody said anything and after a few minutes he got up, turned round, and loped off again, having accomplished whatever it was he came for, if he came for anything at all.

The dogs didn't bear Mr Hare any ill will. Their noses were twitching well but there was no unseemly slavering to get at him. This isn't really surprising when you remember the general sweetness of the Labrador's nature. Honey only growls when Gemma suggests she might like to share Honey's tea, and Gemma only growls if turfed out of a warm bed. The only thing Gemma ever killed was a young pheasant and that was by accident. She had just opened her mouth to remark upon the warmth of the afternoon when the silly creature came bounding out of the stubble, ran straight down her throat and stunned itself on her epiglottis. Poor Gemms shut her mouth sharply to keep out further intruders and thus caused Pheasant Minor's sad demise. Gemma was very upset about it.

This sweet nature is very interesting as it asserts itself in any cross-breed that a Labrador has a hand in, as it were. I once knew a Labrador-Boxer dog that was both handsome and charming and a Labrador-Doberman cross, of all things, which lacked that Doberman inscrutability that makes me want to climb a tree, and had a frank and open disposition.

I have only known one Labrador that was at all nasty, and even that was as nice as pie if one didn't thwart it in any way. On the command 'no' it turned very ugly indeed. It was allowed to roam and used to make a thorough nuisance of itself with Honey and Gemma and would snarl at Jane if she remonstrated with it. One day Jane lured it from the park with honeyed words, locked it in our coal shed, rang up its half-witted but intellectual lady owner and told her firmly that if she did not collect the dog straight away and keep it from roaming in the future, she, Jane, would take it for a nice drive up the motorway and liberate it at junction 17. The woman came round immediately and they had a splendid fishwife row in the street, but the dog never roamed again.

One thing, apart from food, about which Labradors entirely agree is swimming. They will happily swim in broken ice, and the colder and filthier the water the more it seems to appeal, which is funny because Labradors are terrible sybarites and love to lie in front of a good log fire baking their brains, too idle to move until they have to be dragged groaning and smouldering from the hearth rug. The answer lies in the scientific design of the Labrador's functional clothing which is water and heat resistant – a soft lining on the inside which is nice and comfy next their skins, and a harsher outer layer; which protects against wear and tear. A healthy Labrador's fur coat doesn't fit very well and Honey's and Gemma's coats are very loose. It's as if they picked up the wrong coats at a party and somewhere two unhappy animals are straining at the seams, their paws and ankles pinkly sticking out.

When Gemma came to us she had never swum, as her original parents considered swimming in ponds and rivers to be a nasty smelly practice, which indeed it is, particularly when drying out afterwards in a warm car. Honey soon taught her to swim and taught her so well that she was a bit put out at the result. Gemma will leap into water and swim after sticks by the hour. She can't really see the stick but launches herself after it like a great hairy torpedo, setting off at high speed in the general direction of the splash, swimming free-style and whinnying with excitement, with me shouting 'left a bit, right a bit, no you oaf' sort of instructions from the shore because if she can't find the stick she gets very frustrated and swims around in circles looking deprived.

The water's edge is the only place that Gemma likes to hunt and she will crash and blunder about in the reeds for ages wearing black muddy stockings, both she and her tail going round and round, happily trying to snuff out Toad and Ratty.

I realized how fond I had become of Gemma when the soft creature nearly drowned herself during one of our family holidays in the Isle of Man. We had a Manx Tourist Board handout on the Manx Glens which was a glossy single-sheet affair we called 'The Boys' Own Monster Book of Glens', and as a project we visited a different one every day. The glens are very pretty and have a crumbling nostalgic charm left over from the turn of the century when north country holiday-makers flocked to the Island the way they now flock to Torremolinos, and the Isle of Man Steam Packet Company's paddle steamers took an hour less over the seventy-mile journey from Liverpool than do the vibratory modern diesel vessels.

The day that we were 'doing' Glen Helen there was nobody else about, and I was throwing sticks for the dogs down the steep bank into the river that races downhill through the glen, pausing occasionally in wonderfully clear deep pools. Honey got bored when the climb back from the river grew longer and steeper but Gemma kept yelling for more. Finally she plunged recklessly over the edge, lost control and tobogganed down the slopes on her chin, with the wild garlic and brambles pinning her ears back as she gathered speed. The trout in the pool were just comforting a colleague that the stick had fetched a nasty whack in the gills when Gemma came screaming down face first like a cormorant that fancied a fish supper and frightened them all silly again. Luckily she had her mouth shut, and equally luckily it was a very deep pool. Eventually she popped up from the depths looking a bit shattered, but not suffering from the bends, or from having broken anything vital by plummeting down through the undergrowth. But instead of paddling easily downstream for a few yards and strolling out of the water up a gently shelving gravel bank she tried to swim upstream over a sort of junior rapid, and no amount of good advice would deter her, probably because she couldn't hear it over the roar of the river. She went on struggling until she was exhausted and lay there on the rocks, all shipwrecked, with the water rushing over her. I wasn't anxious to go down to the rescue as it wouldn't have been necessary if she'd use her wits, and I could see myself ending up in the water with her. But she looked so pathetic lying there whimpering that I set off down the slippery slope wondering how long it took to alert the Air/Glen Rescue helicopter. I was about halfway down when my frenzied shouts got through to her and she slid backwards into the pool and did what she should have done in the first place, emerging from the water to stand there grinning foolishly and shaking herself.

Honey too had a bit of a drama on that holiday. One of her favourite walks, on a warm afternoon after a pub lunch, was along the coast path from Port Mooar round towards Maughold Head where, if the conditions were right, a colony of seals could be seen sprawling about in the sun on a jumble of rocks, looking from a distance like a pack of old mattresses. If they weren't there Jane used to sit down on the rocks and sing in the hope of luring them ashore. Although she had a pleasant enough voice nobody would have needed to tie me to the mast to prevent me from swimming in to get her, and it seemed the seals felt much the same. Occasionally one would bob up to look at her in amazement, but my suggestion that bunging them a few pairs of Manx kippers might be more alluring was not well received.

On the afternoon of Honey's mishap the seals considered that there was too much of a swell breaking over the rocks for them to sunbathe comfortably without getting their Ambre Solaire washed off, and they were cruising about in the bay when we turned up. Jane, who was in good voice after a few gins and tonic, sat down and started to sing them a few verses of 'Eternal Father Strong to Save' in the hope that they might change their minds, or at least show their appreciation in the usual way by rising up in the water and beating their flippers together, and she had just got to the bit about 'those in peril on the sea' when Honey fell in. There was a nasty undertow off the rocks and although she is a good swimmer she couldn't quite get back. I wish I could truthfully tell you that she was rescued by seals but it was a very frightened family that at last got a grip on her collar and dragged her ashore.

Honey would have loved to have had a handsome gentleman seal breathing hot fishy nothings into an ear full of Irish Sea, and could have been tempted into a watery romp. Gemma wasn't quite so keen on seals, but showed a friendly interest, possibly because they looked rather like Labradors that had mislaid their ears, and because she could see that the seals were fond of water, food and comfort, although personally Gemma preferred her fish lightly fried and served on a warm dish.

I can do without watery romps with dogs or seals, as by and large the majority of people who drown are drowned when swimming, and if I were drowning, which I hope is unlikely as I cannot swim, I certainly wouldn't look to my dogs for help. They regard all humans that they come across at sea as Nature's Li-Los and having a large cheerful dog scrabbling to climb aboard your pink body just as it's going down for the third time could be an exasperating experience.

Honey once sank a total stranger in Douglas Bay during TT week, watched from the shore by a delighted crowd of leather-jacketed louts, all shading their eyes with one hand, pointing with the other, and chanting 'Drake is in his hammock and a thousand miles away, Captain, art thou sleeping there below' until the man bobbed up behind Honey, who was swimming about looking worried, and sank her. I think it must have been the cheers that greeted this cruelty that upset her. She swam ashore straight away and went into the hotel. Labradors have a keen sense of humour, but tend not to find their own misfortunes very funny.

CHAPTER 3

Other Dogs and Dog Owners

Having enthusiastically entered into a doggy lifestyle, we came across a whole new fellowship of people in the park, all of them devoted to the service of the dog. They roamed amongst the trees singly, or in packs, exercising an amazing variety of breeds.

There were no mongrels. It was that sort of district. Not that this fellowship was at all snobbish, representing as it did the whole gamut of income groups from comfortably off to stinking rich, and so long as you were obviously obsessed with dogs you were immediately accepted, although it took ages to find out people's names as they all referred to each other, without being arch, as the parents of the various love objects. I was known as Honey's father, and an attractive girl who owned a fat and lecherous Dalmatian that walked like an articulated wooden toy was introduced as Jason's mother. The thing that struck one straight away about the company was its complete unselfconsciousness concerning the disgusting habits of dogs, all of which seemed to be sex fiends of one sort or another. Having met Jason's mother for the first time, in two minutes flat we were deep in innocent discussion of the bizarre sexual practices that our pets went in for, whilst they, although total strangers, were behaving like hairy and uninhibited actors in an embarrassing Scandinavian movie, refusing to stop until spoken to sharply.

'Darling, *do* stop doing that. I'm *sure* Honey isn't enjoying it.' Honey was obviously loving every sticky moment.

The dogs, although thoroughbreds, were as democratic as their owners, which was nice of them, considering that most of them came from much grander families. Honey's real mother, for example, was Halsinger Atalanta who had been frightfully well connected, for a Labrador. Labradors are really only upper middle-class in the sniffing order; but still that made Honey a lot smarter than us.

The dog-walkers' social whirly burly took place every weekday morning and evening, when the hard core of the daily pack hurried out of their houses and into the trees to romp and mingle. The aristocrats of the company were the Setters: three Irish, two English and two Gordons. The Irish Setters were very beautiful but totally brainless, possibly because there was very little room for anything so ordinary as brains in their elegant narrow heads. The English and the Gordon Setters were much more sensible but not so matey. Other regulars included a Boxer bitch, which didn't look at all upper crust, bullied puppies and went about with a 'my brain hurts' expression on its crumpled features; a taciturn lady Rottweiler who kept herself to herself; a self-involved Basset Hound, with homosexual tendencies, which needed some good advice for the lovelorn as it had a thing about a most unsuitable Great Dane called Ronald; and a rather unrewarding Beagle which was so little company for its mother that she would have been better off with a budgie, although this may have been for the best as the dog spent its time beagling for joggers, and hardly a morning passed without distant cries of rage and pain being carried back to us on the wind. There was a shaggy assortment of Old English Sheepdogs looking much like the runners-up in a home knitting competition for the mentally handicapped, and which must have been hell to live with in wet weather, although I never heard of one shrinking or stretching if dried carefully; a smattering of Dalmatians; several Labradors; and an incredible Scottish Deerhound that would have made a Scottish deer die laughing. The creature put one in mind of a bony grey banana sprung on old pipe cleaners and would have made a good armature for a statue of a very large dog.

Then there was a crowd of Dachshunds of varying sizes and specifications; two reckless young St Bernards that weighed in at fourteen stones apiece and galumphed about at tremendous speed without looking where they were going; a pale-eyed Weimaraner that reminded me of Jack Pallance; a solid mob of close-mouthed Staffordshire Bull Terriers, and a herd of pedigree Bull Terriers both coloured and white. Also along for the jollies would be a Pointer, four Golden Retrievers, Spaniels, Cairns, Scotties and Poodles too numerous to mention, three Alsatians, all hated and feared in varying degrees, and a Chow that fought with the Alsatians.

One could be excused for thinking that with this lot going about their business one would have to tread pretty warily but funnily enough this was not the case, and the fact that there were a lot of glossy and successful-looking crows about may have had something to do with this. Before leaving this emotive subject, I should mention that all conscientious dog owners take a lively interest in their animals' motions as they provide useful

clues to general health, fitness of diet, and to what the animals stole yesterday. I take these inspections very seriously. On one occasion Honey woke us in the small hours of a winter night, complaining of a stomach ache. I dozed for fifteen minutes, barefoot, on the backdoor step while she had difficulty in selecting exactly the right spot, although she had impressed upon us that she was a dog with a mission. When she eventually discovered it I'd fallen asleep. This meant a long and uncomfortable torchlit search and I was just beginning to feel like Sherlock Holmes in the Case of the Missing Fewmets when a horrible sensation between the toes told me the hunt was over.

Dog owning is not for the squeamish, as you can see, and to be honest one needed a pretty strong stomach to cope with some of the dog owners, who were surprisingly few considering the number of dogs. Amongst them were a right wing trade union official and a precarious Member of Parliament who greatly despised one another which was hardly surprising. The trade union man was politically if not publicly several degrees to the right of Genghis Khan – although if you'd have shewn him a horde he'd have hated it – while the MP was a damp left wing liberal; a man with both feet firmly planted in mid air who had made a great song and dance about sending his daughter to a comprehensive school and had sneaked her into a grammar school via the back door shortly afterwards. He never told anyone that his sons were at Eton.

Then there was a Socialist ex-counsellor, or perhaps I mean an ex Socialist counsellor who was all for having nothing to do with the lower classes and who had acquired a knighthood at about the same time that his wife acquired a new accent, although the old one hung on pathetically until it was strangled. And then there was a Catholic priest who was very good company and spoke Erse to his dog.

The oddest of the bunch was a middle aged stipendary magistrate with mutton chop whiskers who longed to bring back the cat and who had sentenced his dogs to long walks. He had a morbid obsession with illness and was writing the definitive history of homosexuality which was to be lavishly illustrated. One pleasant morning the MP who was off to Istanbul to study the workings of Turkish democracy in the very best restaurants jokingly asked the magistrate if there was anything that he could smuggle through customs for him and one of us waspishly suggested a Turkish youth.

Also there for the exercise were a number of housewives, both Jewish and Gentile, a sleek and rapacious lady solicitor, a retired Major, ex Salvation Army, a nymphomaniac and the effete headmaster of a fashionable comprehensive school whose tough and attractive wife was a particular chum of ours. She owned the Chow that fought the Alsatians, and detested them as much as he did. She said, snobbishly, that they were very working-class dogs, although I don't know quite what she meant by that as none of the Alsatians that we knew were called Clint, Wayne or Marlene.

She and the Chow, whose name was Custard, especially hated Satan, a large and nasty piece of work totally in charge of a very wet girl with a very small voice who always referred to Satan as a German Shepherd, a name, so my friend said scornfully, that was used to escape the stigma of infanticide. I took no sides, as neither of my children had been eaten by Alsatians. Whenever she and Custard fetched up against Satan there was the most dreadful fight. These fights could be heard from a long way off. All the other dogs bounced round yelling advice, while my friend obscenely abused Satan's feebly bleating owner in a loud posh voice. If Custard looked to be losing on points she would stop the contest by placing the toe of a green hunter wellie sharply under the enemy's tail, and if you met a German Shepherd on the lead, taking short steps and wearing a support bandage, you could be pretty certain who it was, and what had happened to it.

I may have given the impression that every time one set boot to parkland there was the Tail Waggers' Club milling about on the greensward, bellowing command and insult, the dogs maiming each other and fouling the wild. Mostly one met only a handful of doggy friends, though I can remember mornings when there were twenty-three dogs charging about knocking people over and having a lovely time, but that was unusual.

The middle-aged magistrate was often there, with a pretty youth or two, and upwards of five dogs, all saved from Dogs' Homes (nobody knew where he found the youths) which all chased squirrels and barked incessantly up the wrong trees.

Although most interesting to talk to, and sometimes charming, he could be monstrously bad-mannered and had strong views on everything, especially good manners. His hobby-horses were the spaying of bitches, and guide dogs. Spaying he was for, saying that there were far too many unwanted dogs in the world already. Guide dogs he was against, his views on the subject being original if not sound. His general drift was that it was degrading for such a noble creature as the dog to be lumbered with leading human beings about when the mentally handicapped could easily be trained to perform the same task. This caused many an enjoyable row, although I don't recall any dog having to twist its snarling owner's collar, or put the paw in.

These then were the enthusiastic dog walkers that we knew, but there were others less enthusiastic who were not in the dog-walking set, as it were, while nevertheless walking dogs; a subtle distinction rather akin to the difference between cycling and just riding a bike. Amongst these dilettantes were James and Charleen, a charming South African couple who lived at the end of the road in a house that was either mock Lutyens or mocking Lutyens, it was difficult to decide which, and who owned a massive, eighteen-month-old Mastiff bitch named Gingy, who should have been put in touch with Weight Watchers. Gingy shambled past our house with Charleen and the baby at least four times a day for brief airings in the park. Arriving home one day as they were passing, I stopped to have a word. The minute I got out of the car Gingy growled at me. As I'd only stopped for a chat I was a bit hurt, and looked like getting badly hurt as Gingy seemed displeased at something that I'd said and was jerking her upper lip about, letting the afternoon sun glint nastily on rows of teeth that made her look like a meat-eating hedge-trimmer just back from overhaul. I made a brave try for a light laugh but my heart really wasn't in it. In fact, I had the feeling that my heart was cowering in my larynx, all packed and ready for transplant, and all I could manage was a light sob as I sprang back into the car and slammed the door.

Charleen tapped on the window. 'Den't werry, man,' she said in her clipped Sarth Efrican way. 'Gingy is O.K.' I was prepared to take Charleen's word for that, from a safe distance.

Gingy was horribly spoiled. Nobody ever said no to her, which seemed sensible to me, and she lolled about on the furniture just like our own two dogs, except that unlike them she had a very oily coat, and unlike us they had decent furniture, and the result was unattractive. Not that James and Charleen cared. The day after Gingy had spoken harshly to me, James asked her nicely to get out of his chair, not because she was making the yellow velvet upholstery look like a pair of old overalls but simply because he wanted somewhere to sit down at the end of a long, hard, high-flying, entrepreneurial day. On the command 'outspan', Gingy went into her disguising - fair - nature - with - hard - favoured - growls routine and as she was roughly the size of a pubescent lion James wisely went and sat somewhere near a telephone and rang up the man who had sold him Gingy. The man sounded alarmed and suggested it might be a good idea if James brought her back to the ranch the very next day. Not that one of his dogs had ever eaten anybody but one never knew, did one? Not wishing to spoil a good record, Charles took her back the next day. He said it was an amazing place that simply reeked of Mastiff. There were Mastiffs everywhere, all looking rather like Mr Macmillan, and certainly they had never had it so good. They sprawled about upstairs, downstairs, on the landings, on the lawn and in the flowerbeds. The place was infested with Mastiffs, who all smiled amiably enough but didn't seem to be beside themselves with glee, or even surprised, at Gingy's return. Charles was wondering what they were all doing there, and if it was a sort of prison for recidivist Mastiffs, which didn't make him feel very secure, when a small girl appeared from the middle of a mob of Mastiffs, and crying beautifully articulate words of welcome flung her arms round Gingy's neck.

Gingy gave a long heartfelt growl, and Charles went cold all over. The child, who was all of five years old and three feet high, stepped back a pace and looked up into the jaws of death.

'Don't you bloody talk to me like that,' she snapped, and fetched Gingy a backhander on the snout that made her teeth rattle.

When Charles left her there an hour or so later, she was a different dog. Butter, he said, wouldn't have melted in her dewlaps.

If the dog owners that we met every day strike you as odd, some of the dog owners that we met only occasionally were a great deal odder. Probably the oddest was Paddy, an apple-cheeked and insomniac Irishman who closely resembled a huge and cheerful gnome. Paddy was some kind of antique dealer and lived in a self-inflicted slum that stood in a third of an acre in an otherwise neat and censorious suburb. His house was small, Regency, very pretty, and quite likely to fall down at any moment. In the garden the vegetables lined up in smart green rows but through the kitchen ceiling you could see the sky. The kitchen was upstairs, as the original kitchen, which was downstairs, had got so bad that a glimpse of it would have killed a Health Inspector stone dead from shock at twenty paces, so Paddy abandoned it completely and converted the small back bedroom, which already had hot and cold dripping water, into a kitchenette, by simply chucking out the mouldering divan and putting in its place an old Calor gas camping cooker screwed to an orange box. 'Natural wood,' said Paddy. 'Very fashionable. *House and Garden* are thinking of doing a feature on it, you know.'

It was the coldest, dampest house that I have ever

been in, and on a cold day it was a lot warmer outside. The only form of heating I ever saw there was a fluffy-trousered tomcat called Switzers after a department store in Dublin, and a tatty Border Terrier called Bumlegs after a ballet dancer that Paddy once knew. Bumlegs looked like the world's oldest dog. When he was only a pup and in rude health I honestly imagined he was senile, at least fifteen, and on the way out. By the time he was two he looked like a portrait of Dorian Dog, and from then on it was downhill all the way until old ladies used to knock Paddy about in the street for not having the poor thing put out of his misery, although there was nothing at all wrong with him that a good hiding wouldn't have cured. Bumlegs had a strange sense of humour and if, as he staggered along at Paddy's side pretending to be seriously ill, he noticed a sympathetic-looking old dear he would go into a decline, whimper piteously, and try to pull himself along with the nearside front leg whilst dragging the other three, his eyes rolling and his tongue hanging out, secretly laughing himself sick at the trouble he was causing.

Luckily for him Paddy also had a sense of humour. I was going through a very bad patch of being pompous about the children's education until Paddy told me that Switzer was doing O-Level Mousing.

Paddy loved his garden, which was probably just as well for the neighbours, for had he neglected it, as he neglected the house, heaven knows what would have taken refuge in the trees and undergrowth, especially as the bottom bit tended to be a bit swampy. As it was, the night air was full of strange cries and the beating of wings, but that was mostly owls. Paddy and I shared a love of owls and we were loudly admiring one in his

51

garden one evening when it flew to a tree in the next garden. Jane who had heard our 'ooos' and 'aaaahs' came out to have a look, and when we pointed it out to her she mindlessly asked 'Did it fly?' 'No,' said Paddy gently. 'It climbed down the tree, walked across the lawn and scrambled over the fence.' A lot of ladies might have resented such a remark, but we were both so fond of Paddy, and used to that sort of treatment, that Jane just thought it funny. Not everybody shared our enthusiasm for him, and the vicar, who lived next door, used to make the sign of the cross every time he caught sight of Paddy, which was a thing he tried hard not to do but sometimes couldn't help.

Our friendship with Paddy sort of tailed off from the day that he discovered drugs. We had called to give a bone to Bumlegs and have a cup of coffee, and Paddy appeared grinning and said he was just back from a trip. 'Business?' I asked boringly. 'No,' he said. 'LSD.' These trips were fascinating to hear about and made Huxley's 'Doors of Perception' seem like no fun at all, but when he started smoking funny cigarettes, and a lot of our friends joined in, it became very tedious. If you were invited for dinner you could never be sure that they hadn't sprinkled hash on the spare ribs, and Jane nearly ate a whole lump of the stuff one evening as she thought it was chocolate. This caused great hilarity as apparently it was worth quite a lot of money and was enough to keep her stoned for a month. In the end we gave up seeing any of them, as pot made them talk the most dreary nonsense. Had they been drinking they would have rung up the next day to apologise, but on 'pot' there was no hangover or remorse.

They began to take the nonsense that they talked very seriously, and it had a cumulative effect with disastrous

'a filled kitchen on every floor, in case the current poodle was feeling
peckish . .'

results. Paddy himself had a spectacular nervous break-down, and a mutual chum who had been the best man at our wedding, and who had been a pleasant and amusing companion and a very successful technical journalist, went completely over the edge. He went on a drug-smuggling run to Afghanistan, was caught and put in prison in Turkey and eventually crept home and committed suicide in a bed sitter in Ipswich.

I don't know if it is significant that most of the truly eccentric dog owners that we knew went in for small dogs which were hardly less eccentric than their owners. Not being in the least eccentric myself I prefer biggish dogs, particularly since the summer afternoon at Fram-lingham Castle when I was savaged from behind by a tiny Yorkshire Terrier. That was unprovoked aggression if you like, as I'd never even seen it when it rushed over and bit me painfully in the Achilles tendon. Apart from the embarrassment of screaming the place down in front of five hundred laughing strangers, I got a very nasty fright as I thought at first glance that my assailant was a tarantula. Paddy and Bumlegs are a good example of this complementary eccentricity and equally eccentric was the godmother of Honey's benefactress Felicity. This lady, whose lifestyle was as grand as Paddy's was squalid, had devoted her life, not to a man or men but to Miniature Poodles, not in packs but one at a time. She had a very beautiful house with a fitted kitchen on every floor in case the current Poodle was feeling peckish and fancied a Cordon Bleu snack of Kennomeat Flambé, or quail. There was no rubbish served up round there from a bowl on the floor, and generations of Poodles had reclined on couches and been fed.

Naturally there was a drawback to this luxurious life and that was a Poodle life expectancy roughly the same as that of a Battle of Britain fighter pilot, although the Poodles were never allowed to wear their collars undone. One amorous soul did survive long enough to become an ace by mounting a cat, and bravely persevering when it took off vertically. Felicity, who was a close observer of the action as she had hold of the Gucci lead that evening, said that the poor little chap did the best in adversity but broke off the engagement at the top of a slow roll and spun into a council litter bin from a considerable height. She was all for putting him up for the DSM but he shuffled off soon after to join the Giant Poodle in the sky.

The trouble was that Felicity's godmother suffered hypochondria, and if a Poodle so much as sneezed her fashionable and unscrupulous vet was summoned, in the middle of the night if need be, to inject it with the latest and most expensive miracle drug when all it really needed was an Aspro. Most of these drugs had horrible side effects.

Strictly speaking, Godmama was more than eccentric but despite her little ways and hypochondriacal tendencies Felicity and her husband were very fond of the old lady and spent many evenings keeping her company in an alcoholic stupor. On their arrival a Poodle servant who doubled, or trebled, as butler and chauffeur, would place before them a bottle of gin, a bottle of malt whisky, never less than twelve years old, and all the exquisite glasses, Slim-Line tonics, silver ice buckets and cut glass carafes of Highland water that a person of taste and discernment would need to get falling-down drunk. They were expected to finish off these bottles whilst Felicity's spiritual guardian swilled down colonial measures of brandy and soda and harrowed up their souls with horror stories of the latest Poodle's latest disability. The presence of these ailing animals used to make the occasion really go with a swing. The alcohol used to help a lot if a Poodle, made completely bald by drugs, leapt up onto Felicity's lap for a bit of a cuddle. Even worse was being sniffed, or whiffled at, by a sad creature known as Dr Pangloss since the enchanted evening that its nose dropped off into a box of 'Weekend Assortment'.

Not that the owner of the smaller dog has a monopoly of strange behaviour. The noble art of being a Boxer owner seems to affect some people just as badly, although, of course, it's difficult to say for sure whether the dog or the dementia come first. An acquaintance in the film industry who doted on a perfectly sober and respectable Boxer that had its teeth cleaned twice a day, used to say the most extraordinary things. He was telling a case-hardened duchess of the old school that he met at a studio party how he had bought a three up and two down with an outside kazi in the back streets of Barnet, when she asked him what the hunting was like. He thought about it for a minute and then said that it was OK, but the buses got in the way. It was this same man who was nearly driven mad with impatience in the local petshop by a time-wasting woman who seemed to be doing in-depth research for a flea collar that not only discouraged fleas from dashing up and down her Pekingese's nostrils, but also matched its eyes. There turned out to be a richer variety of flea collars than one would have imagined and when the shopkeeper eventually suggested a Shirley's Dog Band the Boxer owner in him came welling up and he heard himself enquiring if they were anything like the Dagenham Girl Pipers.

If this were only an isolated case of oddity amongst

the owners of a particular breed one could easily
overlook the likelihood that there is a correlation
between Boxer dogs and Bedlamite behaviour patterns,
but the fact that I have only ever known three Boxer
owners well, and that all three were unorthodox, to put
it mildly, seems to indicate that there is some force at
work, some mental interplay between animal and man,
that we do not understand. The other two owners that
we knew were brother and sister, as were their dogs.
Joan, who was a charming girl with money, looks and
brains, but no bust, supported a large sweet-natured
bitch named Dolly, and her brother Brian, who was also
wealthy and distressingly talented, looked after Dolly's
brother Marcus, who was known as Mucus as he
slobbered even more than most Boxers. All four were
handsome specimens but the dogs weren't over bright,
and Dolly was so overweight that owning her was heavy
petting. They all lived together in an open-plan
hacienda on an 'executive' housing estate to the north
of Birmingham, and very elegant it was too, with
polished wooden floors throughout, scattered with
Persian rugs. The only other occupant of the house was
a big, bad-tempered parrot that was let out at parties for
the dogs to chase. The first time I witnessed this wild
hunt I was a little light-headed having spent the evening
in a pub and then been whirled to the meet, so to speak,
in an Aston Martin conducted by a racing driver, and in
extremely close company with a sales director, four
fragrant and pneumatic young women, an estate agent
who smelt nearly as nice, and a Bloodhound that smelt
doggy. As I was crammed in the back under the
Bloodhound, which had supped several pints of strong
ale and was giggling to itself, I couldn't see a lot but
from the G forces coming from all directions I concluded

that the driver was probably a potential mass murderer, although the thought didn't seem to be troubling anyone else, and I was assured that we hadn't touched more than 135 mph anywhere. We roared violently into the estate at sometime about midnight, waking all the executives that the party hadn't already woken. We rushed indoors for a stirrup cup to find everybody standing on the furniture making loud encouraging noises and the hunt in full flight – although the parrot didn't fly, it ran, swearing hard, and the dogs flew after it. The drunken Bloodhound was pressed to join in but lost control of a Persian rug at high speed on a slow corner, crashed into a standard lamp and laid himself out. When the police inevitably arrived they refused to breathalyse him although there was a considerable body of opinion baying for them to do so. By this time the party was something half way between a Tom and Jerry cartoon and the Battle of Jutland, there was a fair amount of splintered furniture about, and the dogs had the parrot cornered in the downstairs loo where it stood on the seat giving tongue. Although it had come up in the world, that bird had been badly brought up in a back-street garage and had never forgotten its humble origins, or the rich and imaginative vocabulary picked up from generations of motor mechanics, a calling noted for freedom of speech in times of stress. There was no need to call the dogs off. They slunk off, embarrassed, and the parrot began abusing the policemen who were sipping Remy Martin to keep out the cold.

There were two sequels to the party. The first occurred as Joan's ex-boyfriend, George, who had started out that evening under the impression he was her current boyfriend, was driving home afterwards. He was waiting at some traffic lights brooding over the news that she loved another, and thinking how much he would miss the dogs, when a scruffy old van bumped into the back of his sports car which took his mind off things. George, who was often mistaken for Guy the gorilla's well-spoken brother, was strolling back to have a word with the driver when the passenger door burst open, there was a cry of 'Kill', and out sprang a big black Alsatian exhibiting all the signs of being in an ugly frame of mind. It calmed down when George punched it on the nose, and staggered back to the van to get a hanky. George was about to reach in to make the driver's acquaintance when the man drove off, which struck George as being rather rude, though he did concede that he may have been in a hurry to consult his vet.

George was very fond of Boxers. Fonder probably than Brian, the next morning when he was driving Marcus to the office. Late nights and over-excitement can be very bad for a dog's digestion, and as they were sitting in a traffic jam Brian noticed that there was a lot of unusual hilarity amongst the other commuters, all of whom seemed to be laughing at him. Brian wasn't feeling his best that morning, probably due to something he'd eaten the night before, but he was slowly beginning to wonder what it could be that caused them all to writhe around and sob, especially at that time of day, when he caught sight of Marcus in the mirror. Marcus was just arising from a squatting position in the panoramic rear window of their beautiful Italian car, and Brian watched in horrified disbelief as tufts of scratched-up pale blue carpet settled gently back onto the parcel shelf. It took him ages to find anything funny about that episode.

CHAPTER FOUR

Indoor Crimes and Depredations

Lovely as it is to own, or be owned, I'm not sure which, by a matched pair of middle-aged lady Labradors who seem to be almost universally admired – they do have their drawbacks, although most of their admirers might find that difficult to believe, having been completely taken in by their 'man's best friend' routine. They once captivated the concourse of Euston station as they wagged their gracious way across it from train to taxi. It was just like a Royal progress. I've never told so many people their names and ages in such a short time, before or since. They had already made several conquests on the train, including the ticket inspector, which was all the more remarkable as they didn't have tickets, and insisted on sprawling right across the gangway all the way from Liverpool so as to be quite sure not to miss anything. Jane absolutely refused to buy dog tickets. As she rightly said, they were much too expensive.

The ticket inspector obviously agreed with her. 'Nice dogs,' he said, stepping over them both to clip our return halves. Most railwaymen are such nice people.

The dogs pretend to think that everybody is nice people and wherever we take them total strangers greet them with cries of joy, making the same ridiculous noises that we make to other people's animals. In fact, we are getting worse in this respect and spend a lot of time cooing over the back fence to the Charolais cows in the field, and feeding them grass from the garden. They seem to feel that this is a lot better than the stuff that they are standing in up to their udders, or perhaps it's just nice to have someone else do the cooking. We even have a pig friend named Oinkers in the farmyard round the corner who is well-disposed to the dogs and comes galloping up whenever she sees us and falls down at our feet to be scratched behind the ears. Ghastly hypocrisy really, as we will probably be cheerfully breakfasting off the poor old love in a few weeks' time. One of the many nice things about being a dog lover is that one isn't very likely to wind up frying the object of one's affection. I honestly think that I would turn to cannibalism before I'd eat Honey or Gemma, especially when I think of some of the repulsive things that they've eaten. Lips that touch Labrador shall never touch mine. There is a theory that pedigree dogs are worse scavengers than mongrels, which I hope is not true, for some of the things that I've seen young Samantha's dog Blodwen eat would have made a vulture throw up.

Not that there is the least hint of their baser natures when Honey and Gemma stroll abroad, smiling up trustfully into the faces of the passers by. This never fails, and we must have spent weeks of our lives telling people their names, ages, ancestors and diet, going into their exercise routines in some detail, and singing hymns of praise to their sweet and gentle natures. The latter, of course, is absolute rubbish as the pair of them are totally spoiled and self-indulgent monsters. If they get the feeling that we might actually be going out without them they go into a heartbreaking double act, rich in pathos and emotional blackmail, that has ruined many an evening as we've driven wretchedly away feeling thoroughly guilty, watched from the window by two cruelly imprisoned tragediennes. The minute we've gone they perk up enormously. Gemma gets the carrots out of the plastic vegetable rack and chews them on the carpet behind the settee, whilst Honey gets on to all the chairs she isn't supposed to get on to and has a good scratch and a bit of a sleep on each, leaving them looking like they have just come out of the clinic for the removal of unwanted hair. When they hear the car returning they leap up; Gemma to fetch us a welcome-home present, like a freshly ironed shirt, to make up for scoffing all the carrots, and Honey to curl up on the front door mat so that she can get up slowly − a look of tearstained forgiveness on her face, to greet us when we come in. We occasionally shout at them for being bad animals, but only for the pleasure of seeing them laugh.

One morning last week we steeled ourselves against the inevitable trauma of pale pathetic faces pressed against the window and went shopping, leaving the dogs at home. 'Mummy and Daddy are just off to buy lots of lovely tins of doggy food, darlings.' Lord Sainsbury disapproves of Labradors rummaging amongst his breakfast foods.

When we came home to a hero's welcome we found the house covered in blood. It was on the carpets, on the fridge, on the freezer, and on the cupboards. It was on the doors, the floors, all over the cooker and all over Honey. The place was like the site of the St Valentine's Day massacre except that the victims seemed amazingly cheerful and in excellent health. A full-scale medical check revealed that the tip of Gemma's tail appeared to have been dipped in blood and looked like an artist's brush. Ever the optimist, I was worrying in case Gemma had contracted a rare disease of the tail, or become infested with tail-eating termites, when Jane discovered that all the silly creature had done was to snag it on a rose bush.

Restoring a Labrador's damaged tail to health is always a problem. As Gemma is a particularly happy soul, having very little between her ears to upset her in any way, her tail is usually thumping on something. The neighbours probably think that we practise the tom toms. Now, apart from just knocking the furniture about, she was spraying blood over everything she thrashed it against.

I did a few sketches, in the style of Leonardo da Vinci, of an intensive tail-care appliance, using a stout cardboard tube eighteen inches long with the end plugged up with medicated cotton wool, attached to a body harness incorporating a central vertical pylon guyed to the collar at one end, keeping the tail in traction at the other. Jame was unnecessarily scornful. She said Gemma would go mad and break up the furniture with it, and very likely break our legs at the same time. I was designing a modification with outriggers to laterally guy the tube when Jane firmly prescribed long healthy walks in open country where there was nothing to wag against, no silly games, and a series of early nights, which worked very well. However, the idea is worth persevering with for treating serious cases of tail injury, and it might be as well to have one, just in case.

I suppose it isn't really fair to class snagging one's tail on the Floribundas as a crime or depredation, but bolting a bottle of tranquillizer definitely is. We only had them in the house because a doctor friend had hastily prescribed them for me. We had met him in the street and without thinking he'd asked me how I was.

'I did a few sketches, in the style of Leonardo da Vinci . . .'

I had been feeling exceedingly evil-tempered for some days, so it seemed like too good an opportunity to miss. Our own doctor, an Irish aristocrat related like the rest of Ireland to the Kings of Tara and now running to seed and drink, said a tonic would do just as well but obligingly wrote out a script for 'Stunnomine' or whatever, just the same. I took two, recovered my normal sunny nature entirely without their help, and left the remaining ninety-eight – the Irish are an open handed people – on the bedside table where young Gemma got them. Had it been Honey, who has a tendency towards manic depression, I might have thought that she was trying to end it all, or thought of it as a yelp for help; but as it was Gemma, who in her younger days was the faintly feminine equivalent of a mindless yobo, it was obviously a naughty badness. Actually I was extremely alarmed, expecting her to turn up her toes and become the sleeping beauty at any moment, and I could have done with a tranquillizer or two myself, but they were all gone. The irony of it was that Gemma looked slightly less tranquil than usual, having labradoriously worked it out that my agitation was probably caused by something she'd done.

Vets are very much like policemen in that you can never find one when you want one, but at least they have the decency not to turn up, as policemen do, just when you *don't* want one. I rang all five local vets and the PDSA. Not one of them was at his post: All out manicuring Poodles' toenails or messing about unnecessarily with hypochondriac cats. The money they charge, you'd have thought there would be one on duty somewhere. After half an hour's frenzy, I managed to raise our own vet and babbled out the bad news. In the circumstances Fred kept his head pretty well.

'Mmmmmm,' he said. 'How is she?'

Naturally Gemma had disappeared.

'I don't know,' I wailed and rushed away to find out.

There are a great many places in a house that a suicidal dog might be expected to creep quietly into privately to compose itself before the death rattle stills its rapacious appetites for ever, and I did a frantic tour of them all, trying not to sob. I even glanced into the pantry, half expecting to see her stretched out in there with the remains of the weekend joint beside her and a touching note, saying 'Gimme eat'. Keyed up for the worst as I was, the shock when I did find her was still pretty upsetting. She was vigorously digging a hole in the new lawn. It was too big a hole to be a grave and a non-medical man could have been excused for thinking that there wasn't a lot wrong with her that a good thrashing wouldn't cure. I went back to the phone.

'Well?' said Fred.

'She's digging in the garden,' I said.

'If I were you, old mate,' said Fred, 'I'd take a couple of calming Dog Chocs and stop worrying about her.'

As you may have guessed, Gemma is pretty robust and seems to be able to eat, and mostly digest, things that would cause other animals to be rushed to hospital to have their stomachs pumped. Along with this epicurean adventurousness goes a pallid streak of conscience that lasts just long enough to make her come and find us and confess her sin by slinking up looking all hangdog, guiltily licking the evidence off her features at the same time. I suppose it's just possible that it might not be conscience at all and that what looks like guilt is actually fear at having gone too far with her dietary experiments. What she may be trying to convey is something along the lines of 'Somehow I seem to have eaten a packet of hamster food and a tube of impact adhesive, and do you think you ought to give the vet a ring just to be on the safe side?'

The day she got the chicken bones out of the kitchen waste bin we did give the vet a ring. Dogs, like everything else, aren't what they used to be. When I was a little lad, there was no tinned dog food, and dogs ate what the family ate, or rather what they left. This included cooked bones, which the effete creatures of today are forbidden to lay fang to in case a sliver of indigestible bone punctures an intestine. Gemma had swallowed a whole carcase. Not that she asked us to ring Fred. She seemed to be in perfect health, but thoughts of having to fork out for her to spend a week in the London Clinic, followed by an expensive convalescence, sent me scurrying to the telephone.

'Fred,' I began.

'Don't tell me, let me guess,' said Fred. 'Honey stood still just a fraction too long and Gemma has eaten her.'

'Not yet,' I said, and told him about the case of the missing carcase.

Fred has great faith in Gemma's tubes. He laughed heartlessly. 'Give the bugger washing-soda crystals,' he said. 'Make her sick.'

I suggested it might be easier to squirt washing-up liquid down her throat straight from the plastic bottle but he insisted on crystals. I sometimes get the feeling that Fred hasn't moved with the times.

Gemma loved washing-soda crystals. Far from their being difficult to administer she couldn't get enough. Fred had said that the effect would be instantaneous. She happily ate half of a largish box. They didn't make her sick but they did make her froth at the mouth. If I hadn't been so worried I'd have pushed her into the outside to frighten the socialist stockbroker's wife and kids.

'Ring Fred back and tell him she hasn't been sick,' said Jane.

'I'm sick of Fred at the moment,' I said. 'He'll only laugh anyway. What we need is something that will sort of wrap up the bones in the great idiot's stomach.'

'Like cement,' said Jane. 'No, I know, I'll make some porridge.'

Not wishing to give Gemma the idea that the wages of sin is porridge, or Honey the idea that crime does pay, they both had porridge. It was good solid porridge with a little milk and sugar and it made Honey sick. Gemma suffered no ill effects from anything as it seems that porridge goes down well with washing soda.

Funnily enough, my mother had a stomach very similar to Gemma's. Not in the sense that it was fat and furry, but in the ferocity of its gastric juices. She didn't test them to the limit by rummaging through dustbins, as her tastes were a little less catholic than Gemma's but she did manage to swallow her false teeth, and presumably digest them, as they never reappeared, which may have been just as well as she could have been badly bitten. Our dentist refused to believe she'd consumed them and fell about at the thought, insisting that somewhere they were hiding in a cupboard, smiling secretly. His point was that her dentures had been constructed at about the same time as the Maginot Line, and from similar materials, and nobody's juices, however corrosive, could possibly have coped with them. But then he had never met mother, or Gemma, for that matter.

With Gemma it really is not a case of giving a dog a bad name, and in calling her Gemma we were actually giving a bad dog a good name. Honey is a good dog with an unimaginative name who reserves her bad behaviour for outdoors. Indoors she is a perfect lady and Samantha once said that if Honey were human she would be a creep. The only thing she ever stole was the Sunday joint and that was Jane's fault. Honey was helping her prepare the lunch and was steadily admiring the neat way the butcher had lashed up the sirloin, when the doorbell rang and Jane went to answer it, telling Honey not to eat all the beef at once. When she got back Honey hadn't eaten all the beef at once but had left quite a lot of it for us. Fond as we are of beef, and Honey, we didn't really fancy it and had omelettes for lunch. Honey had beef for tea, and beef for breakfast.

Thinking of the unkind remarks that I have made about Gemma's lack of intelligence it does strike me that I may have been less than fair. After all, many highly intelligent people do not apply their minds to everyday matters but are absolutely brilliant in the subjects that interest them. Many years ago two friends of ours shared a flat with an atomic physicist. He must have been a bright lad but you would never have guessed. Every evening when he returned home after slaving over a hot reactor his flat mates would say, 'Gosh, Roger, you've forgotten to buy the dinner. It is your turn, you know.' And every evening Roger would say, 'Gosh. Sorry,' and go out again and buy the dinner. Because he was so absent-minded they did eat some rather peculiar things, and sometimes he forgot to come back at all, but it does go to show.

So it is with Gemma. In almost every way the animal is an amiable mutt, but in her chosen field, which is eating, she has considerable success. In our kitchen you cannot hear a hot potato drop, not because it is particularly noisy, except when Gemma is eating, but because she has developed a technique for swallowing dropped potatoes, whole, and steaming, before they hit the floor, a feat that requires quite remarkable co-ordination of tooth and eye and a convulsive peristalsis. Somehow I imagine Gemms's interior as being like the car deck of a cross-Channel ferry: when the hot potatoes come roaring down the ramp, it's all hands to the pumps, or she has a sprinkler system.

As well as being fast, fast on the jaw, Gemma has an encyclopaedic knowledge of the whereabouts of nour-ishing morsels in every house that she has ever been to. Having once found a dying toffee under the settee in Sid's sitting room, every time she goes to Sid's sitting room the area is automatically checked. Before she goes up to bed at night she makes a careful note of any edible item left within dog reach. Usually both dogs stay in bed, our bed, until it's time to be taken out and if Gemma gets up early and tiptoes out of the bedroom, so do I. One morning I crept down after her and met her coming out of the dining room with a new box of After Eight mints clamped in her face. I opened her face, removed the mints and closed her face again. Nothing was said. Gemma grinned philosophically and we both went back to bed.

This is all right amongst family: we accept that Gemma is a recidivist. But we have to be careful how we introduce her if we take her to visit people who don't know about recidivist dogs. Gemma has the ability to go straight to the kitchen in any strange house, taking Honey with her, and the pair of them will leave the car like rockets, scattering the welcoming committee to boldly go where no dog went before, touching down briefly before barging through the front door, felling anyone that gets in their way in their violent haste to gobble the cats' food. Anybody in the house who didn't know they were coming might think they were being brutally assaulted by urban guerillas. Being nicely brought-up they always apologize very charmingly and even people who have been knocked down and trampled on usually manage to forgive and forget, but there are those who brood about such things.

During a successful career of larceny Gemma has eaten all sorts of things, her stomach gathering strength as it matured. She started at an advanced level, at a very early age, by eating daughter Jacky's school report – her first detected crime – which did her no harm at all although the report had upset me very badly, and I had only read it. From that she moved on to tastier things and we have never been able to correct her with severe punishment as she always pleads diminished responsibility. This hasn't impressed one or two of her victims and I have had to protect her on several occasions. The most serious threat to her survival came from her friend Felicity after Gemma had broken into her kitchen before a smart dinner party and bolted down a Salade Nicoise from a huge wooden bowl, two minutes before the guests arrived. I was badly shaken by some of the things that Felicity said about her, and Gemma was hurt and surprised.

Jane was the only one ever to punish Gemma severely enough for her to notice. This was during our brief stay in a fashionable village that had really ceased to be a village and become a suburb. It wasn't even a garden suburb as the land had become so valuable that horrible 'executive' housing had been built in the gardens, a process the planners called 'in-filling', which is jargon for profitable overcrowding. The houses were bought

71

'forming committees to complain about country smells and tractors in the high street . . .'

by transient commuters unwilling to pay London prices. They were not fond of grass or trees and spent a lot of time forming committees to complain about country smells, and tractors in the high street. We had bought an old house opposite the fashionable church and next door to the fashionable pub, and the Rector persuaded Jane to join the choir. He tried to persuade me to join but I explained truthfully that the only key I understand is the sort that opens doors. I wasn't tactless enough to tell him that the pub choir, had there been one, would have been more in my line. Actually I was wrong there as the church choir, who were very good indeed, were drinkers, man, woman and boy, and after Evensong or choir practice whipped straight out of the church and into the pub.

One Sunday evening just before Christmas the choir had scampered across the road and were getting their muzzles into the first round whilst the social climbers from the Congo – a trade term for the congregation – were still queueing up to fawn upon the rector. It was an uplifting evening and long after closing time we filed out into the cold night air singing in unison, not harmony, the most moving version of 'Standing on the Bridge at Midnight' that I could remember hearing, Jane singing the descant. We went back next door for night caps and coffee. I forget whose idea it was to make Christmas puddings but the adage about 'too many cooks' is certainly true even if it forgets to mention that too many cooks have a lot of fun. I also forget the exact ingredients, but certainly a lot of Brandy and Guinness, the remains of a bottle of homemade wine, and the end of the organist's tie went into it, although the tie was just for flavouring and was taken out later. We couldn't find any sixpences so tenpence pieces were dropped in instead and the whole lot stirred in time to work songs rousingly sung by the leading soprano, who had done a lot of research in sea shanties and knew lots of original stanzas, all of which were disgusting but not nearly as disgusting as the three Christmas puddings turned out to be. Not that we realized that they were disgusting and when Gemma stole two of them on Christmas Eve Jane was beside herself. I have never seen her so angry and the family kept a lowish profile when she seized hold of poor Gemms by the scruff and dragged her, tail down and feet dragging, to a makeshift Tyburn in the back garden, saying terrible things to her. Honey was delighted. She loves to see Gemma in trouble and was bouncing about happily, applauding the plans for the execution when Jane rounded even on her.

'Why didn't you stop her, you stupid bitch?' she demanded furiously. Honey, a creature that craves for approval, clearly thought this was very unfair and went straight up to bed in a sulk, whilst Jane laid into a cowering Gemma with a kitchen spatula. I doubt if it hurt much more than her feelings, but she may have got the idea that she wasn't in favour as Jane thrashed the dust from her broadish backside.

When her arm got tired Jane tied Gemms to a tree, started to come indoors, noticed that Gemma had tactlessly started to perk up, went back and beat her some more until her arm hurt, started to come indoors again, stopped halfway across the lawn, hurled the spatula at the demoralized dog, ran into the house shaking with fury, and then burst into tears, having realized that after all the two-bob bits Gemma had eaten, she had been thrashing valuable property.

The story caused great amusement in the village, but it wasn't until Christmas dinner that we realized that the selfless Gemma had been trying to protect us. There were shouts of admiration and delight from a relaxed and alcoholic company when the surviving pudding appeared, soaked in the traditional cheap brandy and flickering with an evil green flame. At the first mouthful the happy cries abruptly ceased and after a moment's stunned silence, normally polite, well-mannered people rose to their feet with exclamations of revulsion and ran from the room. If the first appalling taste of the pudding was an affront to the palate, the horrible cloying after-taste was even worse, and from bathroom to garden the nightmarish sounds of retching and expectoration spoilt the festive afternoon.

When the pallid company reassembled Jane blamed the organist, who was not present, and his insanitary neckwear. She said she was sure that he never removed it, and as the dogs sat down at the table to eat helpings of pudding the Christmas spirit was soon restored by uninhibited speculation on some of the unspeakable things that might have happened to the end of the organist's tie.

CHAPTER FIVE

Travelling with Dogs

I came across a book the other day called 'Couplings to the Kyber' which I assumed to be a sequel to the 'Kamasutra' but which turned out to be a story of a man's understandable obsession with a train journey. I have never understood people without obsessions, having been obsessed from early childhood with wheels and dogs, something which worried my un-obsessed father.

'Ride your hobbies, son,' he would solemnly say. 'Don't let them ride you.'

As neither of us had read the 'Kamasutra' I didn't think his advice at all amusing and went on being obsessed, although for ages I had to make do with other people's dogs and the only wheels I owned were an imaginary set of vast wooden ones that my parents said I trundled about on, first thing in the morning. Railways were the first obsession, which got worse instead of better, followed by racing bicycles and then motor-bikes, a disease which, like malaria, bursts out again just when you think you've got over it. I occasionally buy another bike, but instead of recapturing lost youth it just makes me realize that I am not as supple, fast or foolhardy as I once was and that lost youth is lost for ever. Anyway, motor-cycling can be a lonely business, and a Double Adult Dog sidecar is hardly the Labrador image, and what with the difficulty of getting the dogs to wear full face crash helmets and climb into the panniers, and the speed of modern traffic, I have decided that I would rather go for a good walk.

It was during one of these comebacks that I broke a leg, which was very inconvenient as the family's transport at that time was an extremely awkward motor caravan which had once seemed like a good idea but actually wasn't. It was very useful for carrying timber, but driving the thing was much like steering the *Mayflower*, if not so exciting, although the view from the bridge was rather good. It had looked wonderful in the showroom on a sunny day, and we had marvelled over the way that the cooker became transmogrified into a bed, the driving seat into a bidet, and the spare wheel into a dining-table cum worktop cum washing-up bowl. The elevating roof rose up to provide the servants' quarters and everything doubled as something else. Its shortcomings became evident during a fortnight's family holiday in rain-lashed Scotland where the Road to the Isles looked like the road to Wigan Pier and the vehicle was full of wellingtons, sou'westers, plastic macs, damp clothes, bored dogs, sullen children, tinned food, bad-tempered parents and general ill will. The driving position was ergonomically suited to a deformed Scots Guardsman, and I couldn't even get into the front of it with my leg in plaster.

Not wishing to sit about at home I bought a very old Morris 1100 and a friend made a hand clutch for me. It was simply a piece of square steel tubing pivoting under the steering column. The top end of it fetched up just under the wheel and the bottom of it attached to a rod that went down to another pivot bolted to the clutch pedal. You pulled the top end up to the wheel and down went the clutch. It was marvellous. I shot out into the London traffic to test it, with my plastered leg stuck across into the passenger's foot well, and it was as though I had never driven anything else. Emancipated once again, I could now make myself useful with the household driving chores and that afternoon, with Honey sitting beside me watching out for wild beasts, we drove up to the school to collect the children, my crutches like a keel board down the centre of the car. It was unusually quiet outside the school and the minute that we stopped we found out why. The passenger door opened and an officious female face came in. Honey licked a lot of makeup off it and the face recoiled with an expression of disgust. It reappeared on my side of the car, uttering the tortured vowel sounds of a lower middle-class lady Conservative on the social make.

'Yew cawn't pawk heah,' it said.

'Aihm nawt ectchewly pawking,' I said nastily. 'I'm just waiting for my children.'

'Nawt heah, aihm afrayed,' it said. 'We had a minah accident heah this mawning and the headmistress has fawbidden pawking within two hundred yawds of the school gayyets.'

The headmistress was one of Nature's Brownshirts, who had been a Warrant Officer in the ATS. One of her staff had disloyally described her as a 'roaring dyke' which made her sound like a disaster in the Zuider Zee, and she was quite capable of banning anyone from doing anything within two hundred miles of the school gayyets.

'All right,' I said, unfairly indicating the crutches. 'I'll go and park up the road and struggle back.'

The poor woman hadn't seen the crutches. She went

crimson. 'Ohhw,' she gasped. 'Ohhw. Aihm so fryit-fawlly sorry. Aih had *no* ideah.'

Rotten, I know, but women like that usually manage to humiliate me, and she wasn't a dog lover.

Walking a high-spirited young dog on a lead whilst I was on crutches was more of a party trick than a pleasure and I tried to avoid it, particularly in town. One day I was left with no choice. I had parked the car on a single yellow line and taken Honey in to see a camera dealer she was fond of, and after they had had their customary romp and he had got his nice grey suit all hairy, I bought a few photographic phials and filters and we came out to find the car had gone. Enquiries revealed that the police had driven it away. It had only been there for ten minutes and a parking ticket, to be thrown away and only paid upon the third time of asking when the authorities turned nasty, would have been fair enough. Driving it away was police brutality. I felt like an oppressed ethnic minority. The man who took it must have realized that the car belonged to someone with an affliction. There was no way he couldn't have known, for if one put foot to clutch as nature intended a great piece of steel tubing flew up and smashed one's knuckles. I hoped he would never play the piano again.

The car pound was a mile away and as we didn't have the money for a taxi, we pounded to it on foot. It was a sultry afternoon and the traffic was fast, noisy and nerve-racking. Long John Silver swung along sweatily, brooding on injustice, and Honey had a lovely time making new friends. Dogs simply do not understand disability. Even three-legged dogs get about as if nothing had happened to them, and I know of a guide dog that takes its mistress to work via all the neighbourhood dustbins. Every time Honey stopped for a chat I pivoted sharply on the nearside crutch to cling embarrassingly to her admirers, who all seemed to be meths drinkers down on their luck. By the time we rolled up at the car pound I was anxious to share an outraged Englishman's view on the police force with anything in uniform that was prepared to listen. Had we arrived in a conciliatory frame of mind, no doubt we would have been pounced upon and horribly bullied by coarse and licentious constables. As it was, the belle of the uniformed branch minced out to greet us, fresh down from Kelvinside, and merry if not actually gay.

'Now look here, my good man,' I began.

'Och, is tha' ye wee daawgie, petal?' he asked, flicking a very blond hairpiece out of his eyes. 'Isn't she just adaaawrable?'

He and Honey had such a lovely game that it seemed a pity to spoil it by being pompous, and it is rather difficult to be unpleasant to an effete young policeman so obviously fond of animals.

When he eventually noticed that I was hanging by the armpits from two lumps of wood he sprang up all wide eyed.

'Have ye come fer a wee Mooorris eleven hun'red with a han' clautch, luvvy?'

Here was my big chance to make a moving speech on human rights. 'Yes.' I said.

'Och,' he squealed. 'Ah dew thin' tha's turrible. Fancy takin' awa a motah like tha'. I wouldnae pay if I wa' yew. Ah'd write in an' tell 'em tha' youse crippult.'

We went home and I wrote a stuffy letter to Scotland Yard. A man named J. Chester Stern wrote sternly back. As a gesture he waived the fine. There was no apology.

After the Morris and the motor caravan there were all

sorts of cars. Jane had a sensible family car, and I had a series of cheap and disreputable open cars, the first of which was a Triumph Herald convertible that appeared to be suffering from scabies. After that came a tatty TF MG, followed by an even tattier MGB. The TF was charming, and not all that cheap, but one met such a nice class of people. Wherever we stopped they came galloping up to tell us how they had done their courting, gone on their honeymoon, and had their first serious accident in such a car. From that point of view it was lovely and a delight to drive, with all the get up and go of an invalid carriage, but the dogs hated it. They felt most insecure, and as you couldn't lock anything in it, least of all dogs, it had to go. The dogs liked the MGB little better. They didn't feel insecure in it, just cold and uncomfortable, so I sold it and bought a MGC which was a closed 3-litre version of the MGB which went very quickly and which the dogs approved of, although they would have preferred a mobile kitchen with deep pile carpeting and luxurious settees.

Both Honey and Gemma are excellent travellers and have never suffered from car sickness, although Jane used to, until I unsympathetically shouted at her and cured it forever. Not that they greatly enjoy car journeys and have slept through most of the best scenery in Britain, preferring to roll on a landscape rather than gaze at it. Gemma couldn't see a landscape anyway, though Fred the vet insists that there is nothing at all wrong with her eyes that actually using them, in conjunction with her brain, wouldn't cure. It's just that she would rather use her nose, and teeth. On summer Sunday evening journeys back to London in the MGB, with the hood down, of course, Honey would sometimes keep me company in the front, snuffling up the wonders of the fresh country air and smiling at promenading rabbits. Gemma slumbered heavily on the shelf behind the seats, until we came into the northern suburbs where she would wake up to enjoy the reek of curry and doner kebabs.

Neither do the dogs suffer from sea sickness, but then dogs don't seem to. A large black gentleman Labrador once ate a cheese and tomato sandwich out of my pocket during a Force 10 tempest on the Irish Sea when I was on the way back from the Isle of Man, leaning against a bulkhead on the *Ben-my-Chree* wishing I'd gone to the Isle of Wight instead. He came along all jaunty, climbed up me very politely, and ate the sandwich in situ, using my pocket as a nose bag. Perhaps he thought I might notice and object if he removed it first. Not that I minded him consuming it on the premises. I was too ill to care. But it did leave the pocket unpleasantly full of crumbs, chewed soggy paper and dog slobber, and several khaki-faced people who witnessed the event had to rush off rather suddenly. It proves that breeding will out. The legend has it that Labradors were used in Labrador to swim out with ropes in their mouths to docking sailing vessels whilst the ships' hard-case mates waved shepherds' pies over the side to encourage them.

It was on that trip back from the Island that I learned that the best way to withstand an equinoctial gale, or in our case anything fiercer than a mild zephyr, was to lie down and enjoy it, a discovery made the hard way by falling down to die on a coil of rope as we heaved and plunged in the Mersey estuary which, apart from the lightship, looked more like the Southern Ocean suffering badly from wind. After lying inert for a few minutes thinking deeply about the *Ellan Vannin* that went down thereabouts in very similar conditions with the loss of all hands, I realized that either the grim reaper had stayed his hand whilst he threw up over the side or he wasn't coming for to carry me home after all, unless I feebly tried to get up, at which he made threatening gestures.

As we spent a lot of time, and money, as the paying guests of the romantically-titled Isle of Man Steam Packet Company, that was a useful experience, and if the Mersey was less than flat calm, or Douglas wasn't totally in the doldrums, we got a cabin. Everywhere on the boats are notices forbidding dogs to enter saloon or cabin but the Manx are a sensible people about rules of that kind, and if palms were crossed with silver the dogs became invisible and we never had any trouble.

We never booked a cabin when we booked a passage as Jane said that it was folly to commit ourselves to the expense, for if the sea wasn't going to be rough we wouldn't need a cabin, and anyway, the officer's cabin's were all rack rented out the moment that the boat sailed. If the boat was backing out of Douglas harbour into a heavy sea I thought that was cutting things a bit too fine. I used tactfully to leave the dogs with the family and seek out the hard-case cabin steward to persuade him to find us something comfortable. One horny-handed soul whose hands had got that way from taking 'dropsy' had me rightly summed up as a liberal tipper and showed me into the captain's cabin. It was so luxurious that I was very tempted to take it but decided it wouldn't be wise in case the next time we boarded his ship the captain had the dogs clapped in irons. It turned out to be the right decision, for when I confessed that we had two dogs with us the steward reacted as though I had casually mentioned that I could feel a nasty attack of rabies coming on.

'By the Lord Jasus,' said he, 'come away out of it quick, like. The Old Man'll kill me. He hates bloody dogs.'

Not only did Honey and Gemma spend a lot of time on the Irish Sea, as we lived in London they also spent a lot of time on the road, and had passed a little water on the litter-strewn greensward of every motorway service station between Watford Gap and the Pier Head. They were equally familiar with several more sylvan conveniences off the A5 and A41 and we once had a dreadfully embarrassing experience when climbing into the grounds of a lunatic asylum just outside Liverpool, which we had assumed was a public park, for the dogs to shake their lettuces before we set off for home. Being friendly animals they didn't bother with their appointed business but went bounding over for a bit of a romp with the nearest group of inmates that were shambling peacefully about. These poor creatures straightway assumed that the Hounds of Hell had got amongst them and went absolutely berserk, rushing off in all directions screaming, to stampede all the other groups of patients, whilst we frantically gathered up the dogs who were delighted with the uproar that they'd caused, and left in sweating confusion, pursued by male nurses.

Honey and Gemma have a great affinity with lunatics of all kinds and are very fond of motor-cyclists, and we have to be careful that they don't singe their fur on hot exhaust pipes. They are particularly fond of Mike Van Gee and were absolutely delighted when they discovered that we were going to travel up to Liverpool with him to cross to the Island for the TT. The family were not going on this trip as they were against motor-cycle racing which has become very boring in recent years.

We arranged to meet outside St Albans, Mike on a

thoroughbred Italian motor-bike – the fourth hand-built prototype vee twin Ducati if that interests anyone – and the dogs and myself snug and warm in the MGC, and very content to be there as it was cold and lashing down with rain. After a few minutes Mike rolled up. Inside the car two nice dry tails thumped rapidly and clouds of hair arose. Outside the car a streaming wet machine thumped slowly, hissing and steaming.

Mike handed all his luggage in with heartfelt comments on the weather. 'You lead,' he said.

The second man always gets held up and has to ride, or drive, much faster. Although not a bad chap in many ways, Mike is a hard man on a motor-bike, and he has taunted me for years for 'riding like a bloody old woman', by which he means behaving like a responsible and civilized adult human being. I innocently asked how fast he wanted to cruise and got the answer I expected. Be it on your own 'pudding basin', my old mate.

Time for revenge. Mike pulled his goggles down. Goggles! In that weather? If that had been me out there, God forbid, I'd have been wearing a visor on a space helmet to keep the rain from tearing the skin off my face. Not Mike. He is a purist and it was black boots, black Barbour suit, black towel round neck, a dark red pudding-basin helmet and natty gent's racing goggles. Businesslike, neat, not gaudy. Off we went. The lower stretches of the A5 have been very quiet since the motorway opened and it was possible to push on a bit. The MG was geared to 27 mph per thousand revs and at 3000 revs is strolling along very nicely, and not over exerting itself at 4000. Although the rain was getting worse Mike was still there behind us. The dogs were happily watching him through the big rear window.

They got a bit anxious if he was held up by a car or
lorry, at which point we speeded up, and I always knew
when he caught up. The tails would thump briefly. No
need to look in the mirror, although it was interesting
to see how his face changed colour to match his crash
helmet. Riding a motor-bike in the rain is not enjoyable
and riding a motor bike very fast in the rain is misery.
Mike looked miserable. We were making excellent time
so up near Nuneaton we pulled into a lay-by and wound
down the window. Both Honey and Gemma crowded
to it for a reunion celebration and their faces were all
jammed together, beaming up at Uncle Michael whilst
they wagged themselves silly and huffed a faint smell
of Pedigree Chum.

Mike wiped 50cc of dirty water out of his soggy
moustache with a sopping leather glove. He scowled at
the dogs. 'You rotten buggers,' he said.

Further up the road where the signposts were beginning to talk about Port Sunlight, Birkenhead and Elles-
mere Port, and long after we had given Mike a good
breakfast at a Little Chef and fitted him out with dry
warm gloves and boots, we stopped at a footpath sign
for the ladies to relieve themselves before a long afternoon on the boat. Honey simply has to have grass and
even Gemma, who is much less ladylike in these matters,
much prefers it, and there is not a lot of grass around
the Pier Head. To be honest Gemma is not in the least
ladylike, especially in these matters and has been known
to hold up the mighty roar of London rush hour traffic
by being taken short in the middle of a pedestrian
crossing and squatting down there and then. It is very
difficult to know just what sort of expression to wear on
such occasions at the other end of a shortish lead, when
the spectators are pretty evenly divided between grin-

ners and scowlers. Certainly there was no way I could bring myself to clear up after her with a plastic scoop and a small carrier bag. That sort of thing is really only practical for Miniature Poodle owners. I would have to lug a coal shovel and an evil-smelling hold-all around with me.

Honey would rather die than emulate Gemma. She would hate to live on the great plains of India where there is no sanitation and one can see for miles and the villagers maintain their modesty by becoming invisible to each other in moments of stress. If you meet a friend hurrying into the sunrise as you are coming back, you simply do not see him. This would not suit Honey at all, as she favours total concealment, which isn't quite as charming as it sounds for the minute that she, or her friend are out of sight and supervision, neither of them are to be trusted, and dainty creature that Honey pretends to be, if there is anything repulsive to be rolled in Honey is the first to roll in it. They go in for two kinds of rolling: harmless or horrible. The first is known as 'having a bit of an ecstasy' and takes the form of thrashing about on one's back sneezing and snorting and laughing wildly whilst wagging the rear end and tail, preferably on springy turf or short damp grass. The evil kind of rolling can easily be distinguished in the early stages by the rapt expression; the nose and neck are down, in a lop-sided, sniffing attitude which if not put a stop to immediately, by the loud screaming of threats, quickly turns into a slithering plunge which gets the stinking nasty impacted behind the ears and packed in under the collar.

I don't know who was first in on this occasion as unfortunately I wasn't there to scream out threats. The moment I opened the car door they shot off gleefully their wonders to perform in rural seclusion, and then naughtily misspent the rest of their brief embarkation leave rolling on a powerfully smelly decomposing corpse. I don't know what it was the corpse of, and I don't want to know, but on the evidence it had been dead for some while and was ripening nicely. When the dogs came scampering back they looked so happy that I thought how much I loved the pair of them as they leapt into the car. I changed my mind the instant I climbed in after them and had caught one choking whiff of whoever it was they'd been desecrating. Mike, who already had his goggles down and was ready for the starter's flag to fall, was surprised to see me leap out again, cursing. Actually he thought it was very funny until he got wind of them, and I pointed out pretty sharply that unless we did something about it he would be sharing a cabin with the stench of death and decay, which took the silly smile off his face. Just being in the car with them was like being shut up in a tomb with an Egyptian mummy that was a bit gone under the arms, but there was nothing to be done with them in the middle of nowhere so I drove very fast to the nearest garage with the vague idea of lashing the pair of them to the bonnet and putting the car through the car wash. As it was, the nearest garage didn't have a car wash. They were not frightfully keen to have us either and seemed to suspect us of body-snatching until I explained, and persuaded them to sell me a car shampoo, and lend me a bucket and scrubbing brush. The plague dogs were pleased with their perfume and were most put out to have it scrubbed off. They made me feel like a backwoods Victorian father holding his trollopy teenage daughters by the scruff and wiping 'that muck'

'. . . they liked somewhere comfy to sit and watch television.'

off their faces before allowing them to go to the Hunt Ball.

Actually I was anything but a Victorian father, to dogs or children, and our London home, which sounds very grand but wasn't, was always full of the dogs' and the children's friends. The two groups tended to merge and when the children were little one of our regular baby-sitters was the whiskery magistrate already mentioned. The dogs in his life were a hulking but amiable mongrel, a psychotic Doberman, a Basset Hound, a Bulldog and a spoilt Shih Tzu bitch and he brought them all with him for if he'd left them at home they would have smashed up the furniture. When visiting Honey and Gemma they all behaved beautifully as they liked somewhere comfy to sit and watch television. We had to keep the windows open for ages after they had gone for the dog reek was so strong that even we noticed it.

As the children grew up it cost us a fortune keeping their friends in coffee and cigarettes, and some of the long-legged tight-trousered nymphets sprawling around in our sitting room were enough to make a middle-aged gentleman's hands go all clammy. The musky fragrance of their cosmetics blending with the pleasant scent of warm dog made the place smell like a Poodle Parlour.

Not only was our home full of these nubile creatures, but our daughters insisted that we took at least two of them with us to our holiday cottage to relieve the intolerable tedium of our company. I would have drawn the line at taking the dishier ones with us – I couldn't have stood the excitement of having them scampering about in their scanties first thing in the morning – but funnily enough their company was never requested and we always took two comparatively plain girls with us,

which was probably a manifestation of what a Scient-
ologist once referred to as the Law of Diminishing
Companions.

Because we had to transport these large numbers of
teenagers, as well as the dogs and ourselves, to and from
our Isle of Man holiday cottage every year, Jane always
had an estate car. We disliked the dogs being in the
back of these cars in case somebody ran into us from
behind and so we always spread the risk by having
Honey, the lighter of the two, sprawling hairily across
three girls on the back seat, and hating every uncomfortable moment of it, and Gemma and the fourth girl
sharing the load space behind the seat. I was all for
putting our guests in the load space and making sure
the dogs were comfortable and secure but Jane wouldn't
let me. She said that it mucked up the handling having
all that weight behind the rear wheels, and anyway,
what would their parents think? Travelling with Gemma
can't have been a lot of fun and whoever it was in the
hot seat with Gemma lolling on them, had to be pretty
strong-minded to get her share of any goodies that were
handed round, for at any sign of weakness Gemma took
shocking liberties. On one memorable afternoon we had
stopped for petrol and Jane bought iced lollies all round,
excluding the dogs, explaining to them that sweet
things were bad for their teeth, and they didn't want to
have false teeth when they grew up, did they? I don't
think Gemma cared much, one way or the other, for
when her travelling companion relaxed her vigilance for
a second Gemma's jaws closed over the lolly, leaving
the stick poking out of her face, its owner tugging
furiously at it and being pretty forthright about
Gemma's personality flaws and shortcomings. It was a
tough fight which Gemma eventually won, although I

was hoping the child would win, as I had a feeling that if she retrieved it she'd eat it; toothmarks or no toothmarks.

These rather overcrowded travelling arrangements used to cause problems throughout our holidays, especially when I bought a Citroën Dyane during a fit of economy. It was a nice enough car when one got used to the astonishing roll angles which really required an artificial horizon fitted as standard equipment, but the accommodation was a little cramped and if the Commission for Human Rights had got to hear about it we would have been in serious trouble. If the dogs went swimming there were bitter complaints and they were banished to the back, which they loathed, dangerous or not.

Now that the children have grown up and left home we no longer have these problems, or estate cars. The dogs still have their own teeth and show no sign of growing up. They now ride in great comfort in the back of saloons but I suspect that Gemma misses the swashbuckling days of lolly raiding.

CHAPTER 6

The Dog Cuddle Martyrs

Next to enquiries concerning the dogs' names and ages, and the impertinent questioning of Gemma's sex, the thing that we are most frequently asked is 'Are they trained to the gun?' and our standard reply is 'No, trained to the bed.' Which is perfectly true, and they needed little training as they have a lot of natural talent in this direction.

When we moved into the village, the butcher, who is very keen on shooting, asked us the 'trained to the gun' question and got the usual reply, to which I foolishly added that 'I didn't like killing things', which he wrongly took as criticism and went off us on the grounds of hypocrisy. Understandably, I suppose, as we were obvious carnivores, red in tooth and claw and in his shop every day lusting after meat.

Hypocrisy or not, I don't like killing things, although I enjoy the excitement of the chase, as do the dogs, neither of whom want to kill things, and any small furry that they capture is only going to have its behind sniffed, which might not be good for its image but which rarely proves fatal.

Our dogs, thank heavens, are capable of making their own entertainments. My brother-in-law's Spaniel, which is a pleasant but shallow animal, spends a lot of its time watching show jumping on television, but

Honey and Gemma prefer more rewarding pursuits, and when not improving their minds in the kitchen they practise relaxing exercises. Looking out of the window at this moment I can see Honey stretching out in the sun to keep Jane company as she reupholsters a dining chair in our superbly equipped workshop on top of the coal bunker, and without bothering to go downstairs to check I know that Gemma will be sprawled on her back with her paws in the air, hind legs indecorously apart like Lysistrata about to do a little strike breaking, her head lolling upside down over the edge of the settee, dewlaps flopped back in a mindless grin. They are allowed to lie about on the furniture and they both have very luxurious sheepskin rugs, but come bedtime they are the first ones up to bed, which is our bed, and if that upsets you, it sometimes upsets us, but there seems to be nothing that either of us can do about it now.

All this was Jane's fault in the first place for taking a cuddly Honey puppy up to bed whilst I was in hospital; and our joint faults for encouraging a reluctant Gemma to come and join us. She was very dubious about it at first, having had a spartan upbringing in a puritanical household, but she soon managed to overcome her initial scruples, or disbelief, and in no time at all there were four heads on our pillows, and no paws showing over the sheets.

Before they are allowed up to bed there is a ritual known as 'lettuce shaking' which has to be observed, and on the command 'Come and shake your lettuces, girls', both dogs abandon their pastimes and trot out into the garden in all weathers to pass a little water before settling down for the night. If one or other of us forgot to say it I can't imagine what would happen; they would probably lay awake until all hours looking worried and depressed and I haven't the heart to try it and find out. Now that they live in the country, they love to snuffle up the damp night air which, even to us, is heavy with the smell of grass, and cow, and pig, and no doubt they can catch the scent of rabbit, hare and hedgehog and many other exciting things and Gemma, a creature sadly short of soul, can probably detect the faintest whiff of bar snacks from the distant pub. To see them squatting down together on the lawn, serenely gazing at the sky and enjoying the rural peace, always sends me to bed grateful to be a dog lover, although the feeling will probably pass in the small hours when one or other of them treads heavily on my face, or brings on dreadful dreams of earthquakes by scratching furiously behind its ears.

It was strange that we liked to share our bed with dogs for we didn't really care for having our children in with us unless it was necessary to comfort them out of a bad dream. There were good reasons for this apparent heartlessness for Jacky thrashed about, and being a well-built child could fetch one a nasty biff, while Samantha made wurra-wurra-wurra noises. She went through a stage of trudging into our bedroom in the middle of the night, clutching a vast and lumpily stuffed replica of a multi-coloured Hippopotamus that was called Rheumatism, as it had blue feet, chanting 'There's a 'pider in my bedroom' as she clambered disruptively in with us. I put a stop to that by coming home very late one night, not drunk but having drink taken, and trudging into her bedroom clasping Willie the cat, who thought he had blue blood, and chanting that there was a 'pider in *our* bedroom. That was in those now unimaginable days before we adopted the dogs, which was probably just as well for our mental stability and general health for I doubt very much that a small double bed full of children, dogs and stuffed animals, all acting out their vivid dreams, would have been at all restful.

The fact is that to enjoy sleeping with dogs you need to be well equipped, and lest any nasty-minded person should imagine us setting off for the Sex Shop with our shopping basket on wheels and asking the floor-walker to direct us to the bestiality department, let me make it quite clear that by sleeping with dogs I mean just that, and the Director of Public Prosecutions wouldn't be greatly interested in a soporific cuddle with a slumbering hound, unless he happened to be looking for a cure for insomnia. The most essential piece of equipment for such a mob-handed night life is a big enough bed, and in the early days all we had was a four-feet-six divan which provided as nasty a case of urban overcrowding as you are likely to come across. It really was hell on legs, and the reason that we came to regard ourselves as the Dog Cuddle Martyrs until we could afford a bigger bed. A scaled-up version of The Great Bed of Ware would have done to be going on with, an ambition we probably shared with a lot of other people, as I suspect taking four-footed friends up to beddy-byes is much more prevalent than is generally supposed and will soon be exposed as the social disease of the Eighties that is artificially depressing the birth rate and depriving many good Marxists of the chance of teaching school. Having said all that, I have to admit that we are the only people we know that habitually curl up with dogs, but this can only be because people are too frightened of public opinion and obloquy to confess to it. I'm sure that many an iron-mouthed foundry master, home help and North Thames gas fitter is tucked up snug and secret every night with an Old English Sheepdog in chartreuse pyjamas.

There is much less unhealthy reticence about kipping down with cats. Our friend Bert, for example, unashamedly sleeps with a cat called Meat-axe, so named because its eyes are so close together that you can't get a meat-axe between them. He is not an attractive animal but Bert loves him dearly, which is hard to understand as Meat-axe wakes up Bert every morning by hooking a claw into one of his capacious nostrils.

Bert is an itinerant motor trader that I was in business with for a while, although he is ever such a nice chap and had really done nothing to deserve it. We used to restore post-war Bentleys and export them to America, and because of my business acumen we had five cars expensively bobbing about on the Atlantic on their way to Los Angeles when the American market for them died suddenly, and Standard Steel Bentleys became very popular around Ladbroke Grove.

Bert had another cat, named Sidney, that was feared by vets for miles about and with which Bert did not sleep, as Winston Churchill would have said, not because he was frightened of it but because it was too big. To give you an idea of the sort of cat Sid was, if he met an Alsatian in the street the dog would knuckle its forelock.

Yet another friend and his wife shared a bedroom with three cats named after London greens. One was called Turnham Green as she spent her kittenhood chasing her tail; the second was called Parsons Green as he had a white ruff and the third was called Golders Green as he'd only eat kosher meat. They were much too refined to be allowed out at night to behave like badly brought-up border rievers, or so our friends thought until the night that the tomcat from next door, maddened by the sex, and drugs, and Mahler's Fifth that were going on at home, tired of waiting for them to come out and fight and came in after them, bringing a delinquent friend along with him. Our friends were very frightened by the sudden onset of a yowling combat that made a race-course battle between rival razor gangs seem like a pastoral scene from 'Wind in the Willows', especially as it was brought to them in the privacy of their own home, and they cowered under their Continental quilt to escape disembowelment until the invaders were beaten off screaming for mercy. However much sleeping with Labradors may be generally disapproved of, it must be admitted that large dogs are not given to scrambling in through first-floor bedroom windows in the middle of the night and laying about them with feet and fang.

Not that our nights don't have their various interruptions. Among them are Honey's dog dreams. A cousin of mine used to dream about air crashes and was involved in at least two major disasters a week which finally broke up his marriage. I can sympathize with his ex-wife. Honey has dreams that are very exciting for us all in their own small way. Somebody must have read 'Gulliver's Travels' to her when she was young and she goes in for miniature scamperings with rapid jerking of the legs and paws and minuscule high-pitched barks. It doesn't take a lot of those up against the ear drum in the still of the night to have one instantly awake, digestive juices coming on to boil, under the impression that the wolf is no longer at the door but has used his credit card on the lock.

Another thing that we learned the hard way about getting a comfortable night's rest in a bed strewn with dogs was that the choice of bedclothes was just as critical as the size of the mattress. We had solved the accommodation problem by swapping our small double divan in part exchange for two three-feet-six single divans, and lashing them together, side by side, with aero elastics, which gave us a well-sprung raft seven feet wide – and no sheets big enough to cover it. Either we sewed pairs of them together or converted to the kind of dust sheet popular with the better class of builder and decorator. I really cannot remember which, but what I do clearly remember is that we still had a problem, for whilst the normal length of bed is adequate even for the tallest dog it isn't long enough for me. I am taller than the tallest dog, and rather long when stretched out flat, and my feet still hung over the end of our new wide-bodied bed, just as they always had. The treatment for this was to wrap a big blanket tightly over the bottom of the bedclothes and tuck it in all round so that the first thing I had to do on getting into bed, apart from heaving and shoving a heap of grumbling dogs aside in order to be able to get into bed at all, was to kick out the bedclothes so that they formed a nice cosy envelope protecting the size twelves against cold and draughts.

The one drawback to this otherwise excellent solution was Gemma's dreams, which are much more robust than Honey's dreams and involve adventures with international gangs of dog-food thieves that have to be seen off her territory, and glorious victories over platoons of ravening Alsatians, of which Gemma is terrified. One night the Alsatians joined up with the international dog-food thieves and drove Gemma off the bottom of the bed where she thrashed about hysterically, dragging the bedclothes off us and getting herself tightly wrapped up in them in her panic to get out. I was leading the British Grand Prix at Silverstone at the time, in a hardtop Land-Rover full of piglets and, even over the din they were making, Gemma's frenzied yelping woke me up. I can't imagine what Jane was up to but she insists her first impression was that the followers of the Prophet had come howling down out of the hills and were putting us to the sword and torch. All in all it took us a few frightening moments to grasp what was happening and to untangle a sobbing Gemma from the wreck. After we had comforted her with hot drinking chocolate and Jaffa cakes, calmed the children, apologized to disappointed neighbours who had popped round in their pyjamas hoping that we had been ritually murdered in our beds, and hoisted a fresh head of canvas over the mattress, it was broad daylight and hardly worth the mental strain of trying to get some more sleep. We went quietly about our tasks, feeling faintly unwell, until eleven or so in the morning when the dogs came down looking refreshed and rested, and ready for walks and breakfast.

There is an engineering axiom that if a thing can go wrong, it will, and this is obviously true of beds and bedclothes and we needed to rethink our approach to the problem and find a way of stopping idiot animals from falling over the edges and damaging our nervous systems. Something along the lines of a rubbish-disposal skip filled with Dunlopillo to within three feet of the brim would have worked well enough but wasn't practical for obvious reasons, and even if it had been practical there is something essentially uncosy about a rubbish skip, even a pink one with frilly edges.

We eventually found the answer looming in a second-hand furniture shop in the shape of two huge German single beds, laid down in a Keil shipyard in the late nineteen-twenties. The massive headboards and footboards were all of two inches thick, covered with maple veneer sombrely edged in black and kept rigidly apart by girders craftily left out of a battleship to improve the contractor's profit margins. The springing system was anti-submarine netting stretched over the sort of leaf springs used in lorries and was guaranteed to withstand the ponderous love-making of well-fed Bavarians for many generations. In fact the bed-makers' motto, in gold leaf and still clearly legible on the inside centre of the footboards, was 'You get tired before we do', which had a fine ring to it in German.

The shopkeeper was so pleased to rid himself of the things that he delivered them on a low loader, free of charge, and gave us a decent price for our old divans whilst trying not to weep with gratitude. We got the new beds upstairs after an exhausting struggle, and bolted side by side they gave us an indestructible bed a helicopter could have landed on had it crashed through the roof – and in the event you would have been safe enough underneath it, as the average submarine pen seemed like a Wendy House in comparison. It took up a lot of our room and the monumental dignity of the uprights gave it the look of the rather elaborate 'his and hers' sort of tomb one might expect to find in a Catholic cemetery, just the sort of thing you would have thought that a Satanist Society would have snapped up for their 'après mass' activities. I was tempted to mount a floridly framed photograph of myself on the headstone on my side with the letters R.I.P. carved beneath it, but Jane wouldn't let me. She said it was silly, would spoil the veneer and, anyway, there wasn't the least chance of resting in peace. In this she was absolutely right, which was no fault of the Meisterbed's as no dog, or even dinosaur, could possibly crash through its stout timbers and topple shrieking over the edge to ensnare itself in the sheets. As the heavy wooden bed edges formed a sort of keel or centreboard casing, like that of a Thames barge, where the beds abutted, it was still effectively two single beds and the sheets off our old doubled divan were only just big enough, although they covered several square yards, for one new bed at a time. To save ourselves money we made up the new bed with the old sheets which was just about as laborious as crowding canvas onto a China clipper and was also a mistake, for whilst any animal that came aboard was contained downwards and sideways, it could still bust out upwards, which we soon found out in the usual way.

Now, it may have something to do with our interests but we do seem to have a circle of eccentric friends who keep very peculiar hours and are motoring the silent streets at times when other more conventional, and sober, citizens have drunk themselves gently into a stupor and are fast asleep in the arms of all manner of domestic pets. It was one of these friends who turned up at four o'clock one morning to give me a motorcycle saddle which I needed to finish a restoration. This was kind of him as he could easily have sold it for at least thirty pounds but he was that sort of a chap, generous, and also considerate to a fault. Unlike one or two people we knew who would have rung the bell and been surprised and hurt at a brusque refusal of hospitality, our little friend arrived as quietly as possible on a classic British motorcycle that sounded like two old gas cookers being dragged over cobbles, and leaving it ticking over at a steady roar, tiptoed up the path in steel-capped leather boots, tripped up the front steps, dropped the

'he got it started just in time to escape being hacked to death by life-long
Liberals . . .'

saddle in amongst the milk bottles and smashed his crash-helmeted head against the front door. When I was a little lad I once threw a stale loaf against a front door and the noise it made was appalling, even from the outside. I now know that inside it must have been even more appalling. We were lying there, dimly wondering why anyone should leave a combine harvester running outside the front gate and pelt the house with stale bread and broken bottles when the dogs, who must have been wondering much the same thing, suddenly went berserk. They came roaring up from the depths, accelerating hard and scrabbling for grip on our vitals, to burst out of the bed in full cry, leaving us with paw-marks on our pain-etched faces and the strong impression that we'd been trampled to death by stampeding steers. The herd left the bedroom at a dead run, crashed into the banisters and fell snarling down the stairs to bay at the door. We dragged our shattered selves to the window as all our neighbours' lights came on and our demoralized chum got to his bike, which stalled. It wouldn't start again and we listened in horror to the things that he shouted at it in his frenzy, and the things that the neighbours yelled at him in theirs. It was all horribly embarrassing, but his phrase 'you copulating sow' rather appealed to me. Having kicked and kicked at the bike like a madman he got it started just in time to escape being hacked to death by life-long Liberals in their nighties, and tore off in a blattering crescendo of sound that alienated everybody for miles around for months and months, although Jane went down to the front gate in tears and sobbed out lies about thieves and vandals.

Obviously we couldn't go on like this. The neighbours made it very plain that in their opinion we were mucking up the district and several of them applied for rate rebates on the grounds of our behaviour. As a general rule I don't much care what the neighbours think except when I happen to agree with them, but in this case they clearly had a point. Not that there was a lot that we could do about it short of getting rid of all our friends and both our dogs, but at least we had to find a way of getting enough sleep so that we could be fit enough to withstand the pressures of ostracism and rampant disapproval.

The first thing was to abandon bedclothes for ever and convert to Continental quilts. When we thought about it, it was surprising that there hadn't been a bad case of night suffocation as the dogs used to burrow right down to the bottom of the bed, both winter and summer. The temperature down there was high enough to singe the hairs off your legs, and heaven knows how they breathed. Having so large a bed that only the skin of a long dead airship would cover it in one, duvet buying was a pricey business as naturally we had to buy several sets. I don't care for duvets, but they do allow free access and egress for somnambulant dogs and they did diminish the chances of serious injury, caused by maddened beasts departing the bedclothes at high speed over one's frail body. They also did away with the possibility of trapped animals going mad with terror, all of which would cut down considerably on night-time noise levels for which the neighbours had set up monitoring stations.

The second thing was to go out and buy a single divan of the sort we had just recently sold and train the dogs to sleep on that. But they absolutely refused to do so, although it was moored alongside the communal grave we had all been unsuccessfully trying to rub along in. The divan was named 'The Dogs' Bed', had a nice pink candlewick bedspread, and turned out to be very useful for keeping up appearances with censorious relatives who thought that simply having dogs upstairs was disgusting, and who would have cut us out of their wills had they discovered the truth. It was also useful for putting letters on in the morning, and for either Jane or I to totter to in the middle of the night if it got too hot, or the dogs were restless.

The third thing was to move away from the neighbours, which was the best idea of all, even though it might be regarded as being run out of town. We advertised the house in obscure journals like 'The Rastifarian Hound Keepers' Gazette' and contacted all the weird religious sects that we could think of in the hope that one of them might want to set up a commune, but in the end we sold it to a South African car salesman, who had the money, and five noisy children.

When we handed the house over to him he asked us what kind of dog he should buy his children, which seemed too good to be true. From his specification the dog needed to be a rare mixture of intelligent au pair girl, soft toy and guard dog. Luckily Jane was out of earshot when I recommended a Pyrenean Mountain Dog.

'Thanks viry mech, men,' he said. 'Can you trein thim to bahrk?'

CHAPTER 7

Outdoor Crimes and Depredations

Of our two dogs there is no doubt that Gemma is the most badly behaved, and she is so frequently in trouble that one tends to forget the terrible things that Honey has done and think of her as Little Goody Fourshoes. Seeing them together, Gemma loud and loutish and Honey dainty and demure, it is easy to imagine that Honey was led into misdemeanours by her uncouth friend and has only gone along with the idea to be polite. But the truth is that Honey was born with her fair share of original sin, and when the chips are down she is actually boss dog and quite capable of evil behaviour on her own account. Whereas Gemma's criminal tendencies are directed towards illicit eating, Honey has a wider scope and has been known to lead Gemma into kinds of mischief that never would have occurred to her. The Case of the Courting Couples is a good example which only came about because my one wealthy aunt had a hip operation.

I won't go into horrid details of the operation except to mention that she had it done privately, which hurt her more than the surgeon's knife, as the National Health were offering a poor service and quoting three years' wait. She would have been better off with Fred, our vet, who is very used to dealing with hip displacia, as the surgeon she chose made a dog's breakfast of the job, although he still had the nerve to send in a bill, and two weeks after leaving the private ward she was in a public ward having the job done properly. Unfortunately she was in a South London hospital and this was very inconvenient as we lived on the other side of the river. London, like England and Wales, is divided between northerners and southerners and being an effeminate North Londoner I don't like South London, one good reason being that one can be in Leicester much quicker than one can be in Lewisham, which was where my old aunt was laid low. It was even more inconvenient as Jane and the children were away in South Wales nursing an elderly aunt, so I was on the transpontine mercy dash every day taking baskets of goodies and the *Financial Times*, growling and lurching through the broiling misery of the traffic in the Citroën Dyane, taking the resentful dogs with me rather than leave them at home for most of the day.

The dogs disliked South London even more than I did and could not understand why they were not allowed in to visit their aunt-in-law. You would have thought that a couple of nice clean Labradors, Honey carrying the basket and Gemma carrying the less edible newspaper, would have brightened the place up as they wagged their way through the wards and would have done no harm at all, considering the crowds of unhealthy and unhygienic people that barged in and out without let or hindrance. Not that the dog ban worried their aunt-in-law. She disliked them even more than she disliked me, but it worried me, and the dogs, as the weather was hot and they had to stay in the car. In fact the weather got warmer by the day and by the Saturday it was absolutely baking. On the way home from the hospital in the afternoon, even with the car roof rolled back and all the windows open, the only air we got was the hot wind off the surrounding desert, and the journey took longer than usual, with me at the controls fighting down the 'cafard' and the dogs puffing like wood-burning locomotives in a Western. As we crawled through Hyde Park in a traffic jam, even I could smell the cool green water as we crossed the Serpentine and the dogs were clamouring to be let out, leaping out of the window and into the park, mad with delight and excitement, as soon as I found a place to stop.

The only sexual activity one ever encountered in our local park was between consenting animals, or the occasional exhibitionist exposing himself to respectable ladies, and even that died down for a while after one of these respectable ladies, on her way home after a few sweet sherries at a church social, made a citizen's arrest by getting a firm hold on a flasher's exhibit and towing him to the police station – the desk sergeant said admiringly that he had heard of people having their collars felt but that this was a new one on him – making sure he was properly charged before asking where she could wash her hands.

The pleasant diversions of our sheltered life in the suburbs hardly prepared us for what we saw in Kensington Gardens that afternoon. It was like walking in on a Roman orgy, except that there weren't a lot of metal skirts and robes lying around, for the grass was swarming with couples that writhed about, or slept, in each other's arms. It would have been nicer if each couple had contained a member of either sex but this didn't seem to be the case as far as one could tell – without peering closely, which might have been misunderstood. I was pleased to see that most of them weren't English.

I was very embarrassed at first and felt like the vicar

tripping through this porn field, but I soon got used to it and found myself awarding marks for ingenuity, agility and application. I was just wondering how long it would be before this sort of thing took over from horse jumping on television, when Honey came scampering up and started to play gooseberry. I've told her lots of times that she'll grow green whiskers and that two is company and all that, but it doesn't make any difference. If there is any affection being shown, Honey wants her whack. If I go to make a fuss of Jane, Honey's grinning face is soon insinuated between us whilst the rest of her wags itself foolish and you could describe her as Nature's way of contraception, more reliable than the rhythm method and with fewer side effects than the pill; unless you'd call five pounds a week on dog food, and having to walk miles, a side effect. All these people clambering over each other at dog level was too much for her and she dashed about laughing happily and shoving her great wet tactless nose between lusting faces. I was afraid she'd get bitten, possibly on purpose, as it must be a bit upsetting to be lost in the magic of a kiss and to have the odd sensation that your lover has suddenly grown a lot of unwanted facial hair and a tongue about two feet long that smells strongly of offal. People began to leap up all round with shrill cries of horror, and to stare at each other in disbelief, until they discovered that Honey was the cause of their distress, when they became very angry. Gemma, meanwhile, was concentrating on the sleepers in case any of them had brought Marmite sandwiches along to keep their strength up, and the shouts of the people she trod on whilst rummaging through their belongings swelled the furious uproar. I couldn't understand exactly what was said as most of it, except the swearing, was in Urdu and

Arabic, but the general drift was plain enough. It would have been undignified to run but I strolled away pretty briskly to mingle with a party of Japanese tourists clucking around the ornamental fountains. I tried to look like Mr Nakamura and to watch out for an approaching lynch mob at the same time. Looking like Mr Nakamura wasn't easy as I was two feet too tall for a start, wasn't wearing a smart lightweight suit and two cameras, and there are not a lot of fair-haired balding Japanese about. In the circumstances I thought I was getting into the part pretty well by squinting and showing a lot of teeth, which made my face hurt, and going in for some jolly authentic bowing and hissing. At least, I thought it was authentic, but obviously it wasn't, as the tourists soon turned hostile, and instead of merging unobtrusively I was the centre of attention, my jaw aching like mad, and the nasty feeling getting stronger by the minute that I probably looked like a half-witted Samurai with excruciating piles who was mocking the modern Japanese way of life. That wasn't the idea at all, but they weren't to know that, and the men were beginning to close in, hissing very authentically indeed and saying 'Ah so' in a menacing sort of a way. The trouble is that you can't suddenly stop doing these things although I was starting to wind down a bit. I mean, what do you do when you stop? Apart from run. I was pondering what to do when I stopped, and wishing I was dead, when I was saved by the dogs.

They came flying over the brow of the hill looking over their shoulders and if they weren't actually calling for Dad, you could see that they would have been if they could. Obviously they were very put out by the churlish behaviour of the people that they had disturbed and they needed comfort and reassurance. They got it, too, but not from me, for the tourists fell upon them. I hadn't realized that the Japanese loved Labradors but there is no doubt that they do, and the air was full of baby talk and the clatter of camera shutters, and the horrid gulping noise that Gemma makes when bolting hotel-packed lunches. Meanwhile Honey was hamming up the role of loveable household pet, and the pair of them were very quickly restored to happiness. They forgot about my uncle who was on the Burma–Siam railway, and spared not a glance for me. It would be different at dinner time, of course. I'd be a dog's best friend then. Faithfulness is not their long suit and if faithfulness is what you want from a dog, you can forget Labradors. You need an Airedale, or a Chow. Labradors are much too chummy with everybody.

The funny thing is that they are especially chummy when they are soaking wet through, and when the two of them leapt into the pond for a swim and a romp and everyone laughed and clapped delightedly, I set off for the car before the Japanese discovered that they didn't love Labradors as much as they thought they did. I'd seen it all before. 'There's a lovely doggie', one minute, and , 'Get away from me, you filthy beast', the next; just because the poor affectionate animal, deluded into thinking that everybody loves it, is shaking dirty water over its new-found friends and rolling wetly on their feet. I got to the park gates, noticed that most of the Indians had returned to the happy humping ground, and waited for the screams and yells to break out and two wet and filthy dogs to arrive, all hurt and bewildered, looking for love and reassurance. I didn't have to wait very long. Labradors must be one of the most self-centred sorts of animals that you are ever likely to meet.

The most self-centred animal that I ever met was a

'I set off before . . . the Japanese discovered that they didn't love Labradors as much as they thought they did.'

H.A.G.—E

central-heating maintenance engineer called Eric, who used to come and stay with us. Not that we actually invited him, except by ringing up the oil company that he worked for and asking them to send somebody along to mend the boiler, but they went through a phase of sending Eric, probably because no one else would have him in the house. Eric was a rotten engineer and only stayed with us because it took him days to get anything right. He used to go home at night, but only after a lot of hinting, and almost became one of the family until we all sickened of his company. All except the dogs, that is. Eric was rather smelly and they approved of that. When his constant chatting had driven us to the brink of madness I rang up his office and explained apologetically that we already had two children and didn't wish to adopt a son, especially a thirty-five year-old like Eric, as we thought the age gap could cause problems. All we really wanted was a little warmth and occasional hot water. They were wonderfully understanding and sent along somebody else.

As a constant companion, Eric used to follow us about the house, talking as we tried to work. His worst flaw was his hobby-horse, which was 'good manners' although his own manners were repellent. Good manners, he would say assertively, were not a ritual and it was daft to go leaping up and down like a bleeding jack-in-the-box every time a lady came into the room, unless every other gentleman in the room was leaping up and down for the same reason. If you were in bad-mannered company and nobody stirred, except to make lewd gestures, then it would be bad manners to go leaping up and down as it made every other bleeder feel bad mannered. Eric said that if one lived in a society where nose picking was the norm, and he illustrated his remarks with suitable actions, then you picked away with the best of them in case anybody got the idea that you regarded it as a filthy habit and despised them for it. Eric's theory was that the whole basis of good manners was to make everyone around you feel comfortable and relaxed, and this was from a man who announced to my prudish mother, as he left the room for a visit to the lavatory, that he had to go and dip Percy in the toilet water.

However, it was a concept I quite liked and I wished I could explain it to Honey who had developed a taste for sandpaper. The coarser the grade the better she liked it, which had to be the ultimate in bad manners as neither Jane or I could be relaxed and comfortable as it upset Honey's tummy very badly and she was up and down stairs all night, and in and out of the garden, with one or other of us having to act as doorman and nightnurse. Before we discovered that the idiot had become a secret sandpaper eater we were very worried about her for days, and wondered if she had been getting at the homemade beer which, we had discovered, had terrible laxative qualities. We gave a pint of it to a visiting insurance salesman and the poor chap had to leave the room very hastily, jesting bravely about hating to eat and run.

Honey got so bad that one night we had to carry her up to bed as she couldn't move her back legs and I had to ring Fred the vet at midnight. He was very good about being got out of bed, only threatening to have me put down, and told us to bring Gemma to the surgery straight away. He was surprised when I asked if we had to as it was Honey who wasn't well. At one o'clock in the morning the three of us were struggling to hold Honey still enough to have an injection that she was much against having, with Fred furiously enquiring if our rotten flea-bitten mutt had joined the Plymouth Brethren or something, and managing to inject me by mistake. It was like being speared by a Zulu; I nearly burst into tears. But it was very relaxing, and it needed to be, as Fred insisted on charging me for it. He said it served me right for letting the dog get religion. Jane had to drive us all home in case I was breathalysed. I discovered the reason for Honey's indisposition the next morning when I came across her in the garage munching the pad off the orbital sander, and prescribed a quick clout and a shouting at which cleared up the trouble in no time at all. If I'd discovered it earlier it would have saved me £15 and a nasty wound.

For a sweet and gentle dog Honey has done an amazing amount of damage over the years, most of it in mock pursuit of smaller animals. The garden of our present house has for centuries been a watering place on a cat safari route, which has ruined the lawn. They still pass through, though nobody pauses, and the quicker ones are getting up around Mach I as they flash past the Honeysuckle. It must be something to do with respect for other people's privacy, as your average pussy cat is much better educated in the martial arts than any Labrador and could cuff our two sybarites into an unappetizing blancmange if feeling a little liverish, but they all play the game and pretend to be terrified. Or could it be that they have a sense of humour and enjoy the yells, and the sounds of breaking glass and furniture, as the Guardians of the Pass thunder out to get them? Honey has been known to come through the chicane from the dining room completely out of control, to collide with their water bowl and smash it to pieces, flooding the kitchen floor, before accelerating away in a flurry of growls and wheelspin to protect her outside interests. Gemma, still dazed from a high-speed crash with a coffee table, arrived in the kitchen going eyeballs out and impossibly fast, heeled over well beyond the limits of adhesion for dry lino tiles. She got onto the wet tiles before we had time to put warning flags out and aquaplaned backwards through the doors of the sink unit with the entire family screaming out warnings and threats. I should think that generations of kittens have giggled themselves silly over that.

It is strange that such a nice-minded animal as our Honey hasn't confined her talent for destruction to the house and garden, but on two occasions has managed to injure people quite seriously, although nothing was further from her thoughts. I don't mean knocking smartly dressed strangers flat in the mud whilst romping in the park with a dashing admirer; that can happen to any high-spirited and healthy dog, though people can get amazingly stuffy about it. No, this was real life drama involving hospitals and ambulances and all kinds of upset that have not been at all amusing.

The first time she tasted human blood, as it were, was at Port Cornaa in the Isle of Man where we were walking the dogs on the Barony Estate and came across a brood of ducklings paddling about with their mum on a very small pond. Whilst most of us were going 'oooh' and 'aaah' over them, young Samantha, who must have been about ten years old at the time, had the sense to put Honey on the lead as she knew what would happen when Honey saw them. Gemma wouldn't see them unless somebody told her about them. Unfortunately when Honey did see them it happened just the same and she took off, all anxious to be a baby duck's auntie and have a lovely game with them in the water.

Samantha, having the lead wrapped round her wrist, went some of the way with Honey, and came down teeth first on a boulder, and there were blood, tears, and cuddles, and a fast drive to Nobles Hospital in Douglas. Honey was terribly upset about it but there wasn't time to comfort her too in the heat of the action. Luckily the teeth were only loosened. A very competent dentist splinted them up, and a few months afterwards they were as strong and white as ever and Samantha, who is almost as nice-minded as Honey, never blamed her for a moment.

A few months after that Honey pulled my elderly mother over and dislocated her shoulder, but at least she kept it in the family and nobody sued us. As mother weighed all of six stones, and wasn't significantly taller than Honey, she shouldn't really have been holding the lead at all, but she was an obstinate old lady and had insisted on taking Honey up the road to post a letter, or to be more precise, the arrangement was for Honey to carry the letter up the road, and for Mother to post it. On the way there they met a well set-up young Boxer that Honey lusted after, and spitting out the letter she made a lunge at him to do something personal, pulling Mother's arm from its socket. Mother was not as nice-minded as Honey or Samantha and blamed me for it. She said very firmly that Honey was badly brought up.

I had to admit that there might be something in what she said. I was, after all, sitting beside her bed of pain in the local cottage hospital as she lectured me on the subject and it seemed more tactful to admit it. And mother had been present when Honey brought disgrace upon herself and her family at a picnic in Windsor Great Park.

We were picnicking there 'on fambly' partly because

the dogs enjoy a good picnic and partly because my mother was staying with her sister who lived nearby. I was fond of my uncle and aunt, and would have been even fonder of them had they allowed our dogs into their house, but somehow or other they had become over fastidious and semi-detached proud. Actually, they were not over-keen on allowing *me* in their house as I was heavily tainted with dog but, so long as I promised not to moult, and removed every last germ-infested dog's hair from my socks and underwear, I was tolerated for a while, provided I sat quietly and agreed that the district, and the country, were going to the dogs.

Their garden was as highly polished as their house and they had unilaterally extended their territorial boundaries to include the strip of grass between the pavement and the road outside, and this grass was neatly mown and heavily defended against incursion by neighbours who regarded it as No Man's Land. If a neighbour's dog defiled it there was uproar and the dog's owners were pursued, or called upon, and formally presented with the results of their doggie's best endeavours on a coal shovel that was kept for this purpose. This shovel had a specially sharpened leading edge, and whenever I was allowed in the house I always expected to see it simmering in a stainless steel sterilizer on the sideboard.

It was better really not to visit the house, as it was so clean it made one feel slightly insanitary, and it wasn't very restful with Uncle constantly patrolling at the window. You would have thought that the Mau Mau were out there. The neighbours regarded the whole thing as a huge joke and used to imitate bugle calls whenever Uncle appeared and were always sneaking strange deposits onto the disputed grass, under cover of darkness and their front walls, from a plastic container lashed to the end of a fifteen-foot bamboo pole from the centre of a roll of carpet. Some of the things that Uncle found out there should have made it obvious to him that somebody local had access to a zoo, or a circus, and was having him on. I once asked him, as he puzzled over the origins of a particularly impressive mound, which of the neighbours kept a rhinoceros, but he thought I was just being frivolous and attributing it to a giant Poodle that lived at the end of the road, struggled off up there with the droppings in a bucket and had a tremendous row.

The picnic was planned as the most tactful way of avoiding this kind of unpleasantness and went off rather well considering the nervous tension, and physical effort, involved in keeping Gemma from dribbling on Auntie's tweeds. Having got through assorted pies, puddings and sandwiches, and a couple of litre bottles of supermarket dry white, we were relaxing in the dappled sunlight under the trees; the dogs, satisfied that there was absolutely nothing left to eat, had gone to explore, Jane was reading Gerard Manley Hopkins, Uncle was sketching the plans for an anti-Poodle mine on the back of a paper plate, the children were playing happily, and life didn't seem so bad after all. Until Honey reappeared looking extremely pleased with herself, having lunched alfresco on something disgusting she'd found in the bushes. Smiling a green and stinking smile she trotted straight up to Auntie and began licking her face. I honestly thought that Auntie's mind would snap with the horror of it, for mine was reeling a bit and it wasn't my face she was licking. But Auntie fought back strongly with the tea cosy she was knitting and started a long thin scream, and the long thin scream of a retired music teacher can be a moving experience. It certainly moved us all to drag Honey away, and while we comforted the poor woman, who was pleading to be taken home to have her head boiled in Dettol, Jane was cleaning Honey's teeth with a twig and telling her that she had let the side down. But the afternoon was ruined. Relations with that branch of the family have never been the same since, and nobody has ever been able to explain what made Honey do such a thing. Probably the same mysterious force that makes cats excessively friendly to people who are allergic to them.

One thing that can be said in Gemma's favour is that she has never seriously injured anybody, not physically that is, though she can fetch you a bad scratch on the leg if she feels like a silly game. This may be bad for tights and temper but you'd hardly call it GBH or Malicious Wounding. She has inflicted some pretty severe mental damage, though, and the occasion that she drank the fisherman's tea is etched on my psyche. Luckily he wasn't the sort of butch and bearded fisherman camping about in sou'wester and waders and armed with net and gutting knife, but you could see he was the sort of fisherman who was best left alone, as he was large and hard featured and had an aura of brooding hostility. Why Gemma had to pick on his tea I can't think. The canal bank was crawling with poor physical specimens with glasses and retiring natures, all of them guzzling tea like mad. I could have kicked sand in their faces if they had turned nasty. Gemma had to get her face into a cup of tea belonging to the one man for miles who looked as though he enjoyed pulling the arms off dog lovers. She made such a filthy racket slurping at it that he turned round and saw us. It was all right for her. She shot off to a safe distance leaving me to laugh it off, which turned out to be a bad mistake as he didn't find it at all funny and became quite explicit with the blunt end of a nasty looking fishing rod. It was soon very obvious that he wanted blood much more than the apologies I was bleating out. I was so frightened I actually gibbered. Honey, to her credit, did stay with me but, peeking out nervously from behind my legs, she wasn't exactly disguising furry nature with hard-favoured rage, and when the brute lunged for me she didn't sink her teeth into his leg, or anything practical like that. Just gave a squeak when I stepped back on her, and then joined me in a headlong flight, yelping with terror and getting under my feet, while up ahead the other hard-case hound was legging it for safety. A couple of Pekingese would have been more use in the circumstances, and probably wouldn't have gone in for stealing a violent criminal's afternoon tea in the first place. Maybe a few years in Broadmoor had left him a little out of condition, or I could run a lot faster than I thought I could. We managed to escape whatever it was he had in mind for us. All very upsetting, thanks to Gemma, but at least there was no loss of face, or teeth, involved. The dogs regard abject cowardice in the face of danger as perfectly reasonable behaviour, which is very sensible of them. You don't hear of many Labradors being posthumously awarded the DSM, and I don't suppose this worries them one bit.

People who for the first time have watched Gemma eat, and are just getting over it, often ask us if she would eat herself to death, given the opportunity, and our answer is 'Yes, she would'. We don't just think so, we know that she would, because the day she found the 'Long-dead Sheep' she very nearly managed it. We were on a camping holiday in North Wales, beside a

'. . . he wanted blood much more than the apologies I was bleating out.'

salmon river and first thing one morning we were watching the fishermen jumping and the salmon ignoring them when Gemma slunk away. The farmers in those parts tend to be a bit trigger-happy when strange dogs get amongst their sheep. Not that Gemma would worry a sheep, as she was far too busy worrying us, but you couldn't expect a farmer to realize that and we frantically organized a family search party. To be truthful, only Jane and I were frantically searching and the children were tottering about in a resentful daze having been hauled out of bed, but there was always the slim chance that they might trip over her. We had a bad half-hour before we came across her gorging herself on what had been a largish corpse of mutton, and by the smell of the pair of them it was clearly not a recent bereavement. I reckon we got there just in time to save her life. She was absolutely vast and another two mouthfuls would have finished her off. I dragged her away from the carcase by her tail which was as close as I wanted to get to her and said things that I was sorry for later on, but I did fight down a desire to kick her behind as I could see she could very well burst. I've never seen a dog so stupefied with food, even at Christmas, but she wasn't too stupefied to realize that for some reason or other she wasn't dog of the month in our book and might be safer elsewhere. It was like watching a well fed vulture trying to take off. By the time I got back to the tent Gemma had collapsed. She was ill for days, and unpleasant company, lying about on her back with her legs sticking stiffly up in the air and her stomach in turmoil, groaning a lot. The groaning got on my nerves to such an extent that I was all for moving her into the children's tent and having them in with us, but Jane wouldn't hear of it. She nursed the great glutton through the fermentation period by rubbing her tummy and murmuring 'there, there', which was even more irritating than the groaning. What really annoyed me was that when I had a hangover, which was all Gemma was really suffering from, nobody rubbed my tummy and murmured, 'there, there'. It would probably have driven me mad if they had but that wasn't the point.

The thing that really thickened up the scar tissue of my soul was Gemma's numerous abscondings. When she was young she was terrible. If you took your eyes off her for a moment she would disappear to plunder the neighbourhood dustbins and not come back for hours. Eaten up with angst I used to get the car out and slowly cruise the streets looking for her. It's a miracle that I wasn't arrested for soliciting. I only ever caught her once, when I came slowly round a corner to find her crossing the road keeping company with a Corgi named Cuthbert who was wearing brown and white co-respondent shoes and a thin moustache and looking very pleased with himself. Gemma started guiltily when she saw me, so you can tell that she knew she was being a bad animal, and Cuthbert melted quickly away. His duties as a gigolo didn't extend to having his behind kicked by a furious father.

Gemma got a beating that time, but not serious enough to have any lasting effect, as it is difficult to beat a dog satisfactorily whilst kneeling on the driving seat of a sports car with the hood up, the victim burrowing down behind the seat mumbling prayers.

If she got home without being apprehended we were so pleased to see her that she usually got cocoa and biscuits instead of the whacking she richly deserved, as there is no point in belabouring a dog when it trots home of its own volition looking all penitent.

It wasn't that I doubted that she would come home if she could. It was the 'if she could' bit that worried me silly. We lived in a quiet haven in the middle of a whirling maelstrom of traffic and Gemma had all the road sense of a geriatric baboon. The worst row I ever had with Jane was over Gemma slinking off while Jane was in charge of her. The really worrying thing was that she was two miles from home when Gemma went missing, on a dark, wet, Friday evening in the rush hour. Jane hunted for her for an hour; Honey was no help on these occasions, she just looked blank when instructed to go and find Gemma. Jane then came home in tears to tell me about it. Very unreasonably, since it could just as easily have happened to me, I went berserk. To get home Gemma would have to cross a road so busy that it was virtually impossible to cross, without walking miles in either direction to pedestrian crossings where you were a little less likely to get mown down so long as you were nimble. Somehow I couldn't see Gemma doing that. The Green Cross Code meant about as much to her as Lateral Thinking. If she wanted to cross the road, she crossed. I went up there in the car and toured around trying not to sob, convinced I'd seen the last of the daft mutt. Alive, that is. I quite expected to find her pathetic body in the gutter at any minute. In the end I went home in despair and sat miserably drinking a good malt whisky, which was a terrible waste, and wondering if Gemma would rather be cremated or buried, moving on to ponder on methods of suicide. I rejected the impulse to slit my throat when I remembered I only had an electric razor; the idea was to end it all, not punish myself.

A dog-walking chum brought Gemma home. She was articulating in all limbs and in the over-affectionate sort of mood that turneth away a good hiding. How she crossed that dreadful road I will never know, but I think she must have had some very nasty moments, as the friend who brought her home said that Gemma had dashed up to him in the park and fallen down at his feet in floods of tears. She hasn't run away for years. But I still don't trust her.

CHAPTER 8

Names and Games

Now that we live next door but one to the village butcher Jane often threatens Gemma that she will be sent off to him to be made into sausages, which Gemma thinks is very funny. 'Right. That's it. Off to Stumpy,' is the punishment for minor crimes like chewing slippers, or eating the bread put out for the birds.

Mr Stump, the butcher, has in fact got his full complement of limbs, which in a village like ours is just as well, for had he lived up to his name and lost one there would have been evil rumours circulating about his fillet end of leg. He was the butcher who went off us on the grounds of hypocrisy but, luckily for us, got over it before we took um and flounced off to take our custom elsewhere, and so missed out on his theories about being under dogged or over dogged that he told us about over a pint in the public bar of 'The Fox' the day that he decided we were chums again. He said that in his experience it was very difficult not to be one or the other. If you were under dogged with just one dog and went out and got another dog, as two dogs is about the right number of dogs to have, then the first dog would have puppies, or somebody would leave you a dog in their will, or a dog would turn up, all pathetic, on your doorstep and ask to be adopted, and there you were: over dogged.

I can't say it's something that we have suffered from, but young Samantha has managed to be over dogged just by having Blodwen. Blodwen has the energy of fourteen dogs and no sense of proportion, a phrase that my parents were fond of although I never knew what it meant until Blodwen turned up without one. The first time she came to our new home she was so excited that she sprang, barking, onto the table and did several laps of the room on the tops of the furniture, bit Jane on the hand, put a foot through my watch glass, and when screamed at to stop, took up a foetal position under the wreck of the sideboard, convinced that nobody loved her.

Samantha got Blodwen as a substitute for a puppy that came to stay one night. I had opened the back door to let the dogs out and the puppy had walked in. Its pedigree must have read like something by Bram Stoker but it was so sweet that even Honey and Gemma liked it, and Samantha fell in love with it and took it off to bed with her to tell it a bedtime story, as soon as it had had its supper. We all assumed that the poor little thing had been cruelly abandoned, the unwanted child of a single-parent family, but there was a bit of a heart-break in the morning when somebody told us that the puppy lived with an American family in an impossibly grand house round the corner. Unfortunately they described the wrong impossibly grand house and with the pup bouncing about on a lead we walked right past its owner when I went to take it home. Standing in a front garden that was heavy with the scent of hominy grits and cannabis was a large coloured lady who was tongue-lashing a group of white trash that turned out to be her employers. A sudden hush fell as we trotted past but I didn't think a lot about it until a voice that made Paul

Robeson sound like a castrati said *'Dats mah dawg'* and eighteen stone of cook and housemaid dashed past to snatch up the pup and cuddle it to bits. I thought for a moment that she was going to sing it a selection from 'Porgy and Bess', and the puppy seemed to think so too as it was writhing a lot and looking pretty restive at all the Southern comfort it was getting. All I was getting was suspicious looks but I did convince her in the end that I had only been trying to do the decent thing. Then I slunk off home feeling like a dog-stealing carpet-bagger caught with his bags down and not at all sure that I'd done the right thing. Twenty minutes later as we were driving down to the shops I was convinced that I hadn't when the puppy I'd just taken home shot out of the hedge and scampered across the road in front of us.

We were always taking wandering dogs home, and often people used to look at us as if we were mad, say 'Oh. Thanks,' rather absently and let the dog go again the minute we'd driven off. Americans seemed to be the worst offenders at this. Somebody told us that packs of uncared-for dogs roamed American streets as herds of buffalo once roamed the plains. Actually I could believe it. An American couple who rented a house nearby had the most beautiful yellow Labrador pup that was allowed to wander, even when it was so small it could have been mugged by mice. I was always retrieving this jolly little soul from the traffic and taking it home, becoming progressively more offensive to its owners about their heartless stupidity, but it didn't make any difference. Not really surprising, as the husband went in for bright green suits, the wife was an unbelievably skinny ash blonde who thought that anorexia was an obsessional fear of anoraks, and had majored in sociology, and their au pair girl had been highly trained at a camp in Albania on the latest techniques in mucking up the simplest telephone message.

We were tempted to set up an underground organization along the lines of the wartime 'Lifeline' in occupied France, to smuggle out dogs in moral and physical danger to good homes in the country. But I doubt if it would have worked as people can be so picky. They wouldn't simply have given a good home to a dog that needed it, and you could have turned up all clandestine at a 'safe house' in the middle of the night with an exhausted King Charles Spaniel under your trenchcoat and they would have said, 'Not today, thanks. We wanted a three year-old Harlequin Great Dane bitch, fond of children and travel, and not too fussy about its food.' And you try finding one of those in distress, never mind getting it under your trenchcoat. We were not proposing to become full-time dog-stealers.

Samantha was terribly upset at the loss of her puppy and insisted on going to Battersea Dogs Home to get a replacement. Blodwen was the result. I tried to dissuade her by promising to buy her a pedigree pup. That way at least you know what sort of trouble to expect, but I was accused of snobbishness and elitism. Blodwen made the central character of 'Your Baby Has Gorn Down the Plug 'Ole' sound astoundingly robust, and Honey and Gemma snobbishly and uncharitably hated her from the start. They could see that she wasn't out of the top drawer, or even the bottom drawer, but had been dragged out from under the furniture and foisted on my daughter. Blodwen has a very nice smile and Samantha has a very soft heart.

Why Blodwen was named Blodwen I can't tell you. I

was walking with her in the park one evening – Honey and Gemma had gone off pretending they weren't with us – when we met a middle aged duchess and three Pekingese who all goggled a bit when I called out for Blodwen, and I admitted to them that I thought Blodwen was a silly name for a dog to have. The duchess said bluntly that she thought that Blodwen was a bloody silly name for *anybody* to have and went on a bit about the silly names that people gave to pets. I was worried in case Blodwen's doting mother came along and heard her, as we seemed to be going through a healthily outspoken Punk Marxist phase at the time and would have enjoyed being offensive to a symbol of an outdated social order. In fact there could very well have been an ugly scene if Samantha hadn't been knocked over by a gambolling Great Dane bitch named Marlene as she walked across the park to meet us, turning up all white and wobbly with a story about Marlene licking her face as she lay stunned, which I believed, and trying to take her pulse, which I wasn't so sure about.

Naming dogs is very difficult but naming children is even worse, as one likes a lot more dogs than one likes people and nobody wants to give their child a name that reminds them of somebody that they despise. And you can hardly name your boys Bonzo and Rover after a couple of mongrels you were fond of, but you can call your dogs Mark and Crispin, although for a bitch I think I'd prefer Lassie or Patch to Doreen, as I've never known anybody called Lassie or Patch.

Only yesterday we met a handsome black dog – I suppose it might be more delicate to say coloured but that could mean that he was grey, white and ginger – whose name was Hudson, because Hudson was near Labrador and so was he, and we once knew a Labrador named 'Stinky Wogle' another name I wouldn't give a child, as it got abbreviated to Stinks. Some of the affectionate names that we have called Honey and Gemma have been little better and would have beggared a non-dog-lover's belief. For some reason or another we went through a phase, when the children were quite small, of calling the dogs Honey Woggis and Gemma Woggis, or referring to them collectively as The Woggises. One day a snooty little chum of Samantha's was sneering at our Volkswagen – her father drove a Jaguar, very badly – and asked what VW meant anyway, and quick as a flash young Sam said 'Vera Woggis' and went off into hysterics. I was proud of her, and her idea of a joke must tell you something about the importance of environment in a child's upbringing, as nobody could possibly be born as silly as that.

Some years ago outside a pub in Cheshire, we briefly made the acquaintance of a very noble yellow Labrador called Claude who was unmistakably a gentleman of the old school, which is more than can be said for our local pub cat who was called Susie for months until a lady who was rubbing Susie's tummy discovered that Stanley would have been a more suitable name. When I say 'old school' I mean that Claude was the old fashioned, utterly confident, sort of Labrador, big enough to make a well nourished Mastiff look like a seven stone weakling. We fell in love with him instantly, although having a pair of dogs like him would have meant moving to a larger house and changing our car and milkman, as our car would have been much too small and the milkman was already frightened of Honey, and absolutely terrified of Gemma. I think that he suffered from an irrational dread of being licked to death, and he shook so much as he came up the path that we quite often got two pints of cheese. Two dogs like Claude would have curdled his yoghourt.

Claude arrived unassumingly in a dark green Aston Martin convertible with two audibly upper crust ladies who were probably mother and daughter as they looked rather alike and loudly addressed each other as 'Penelope doorling' and 'Mummy doorling'. Claude wasn't a 'doorling', he was a 'sweetie'. I love other people's conversations but these two had everybody's attention as their decibel output was completely uninhibited and could have made them liable to prosecution on the grounds of noise pollution. I don't mean this unkindly as they were obviously pleasant people but they did impinge.

As it was such a lovely day – 'Such a *lovely* day, Mummy doorling. *Do* let's sit in the garden' – they settled at a table in the garden, after deciding that several other tables were quite unsuitable. They agonized about 'drinkies' to such an extent that everybody began to wonder if they'd make up their minds and get to the bar before closing time, and there was some speculation that they might be expecting a waiter. It was a great relief to us all when they decided on two rather good dry sherries and Penelope, who moved very nicely like Joan Hunter Dunn, went off to get them. She came back immediately without the drinks, having sensibly realized that should Claude, who seemed to have much the same plebeian appetites as lesser Labradors, take it into his magnificent broad head to pay a social call to a bitch on heat then Mummy would have to go with him as she certainly wouldn't be able to stop him. I could just imagine Mummy. 'Claude. Sweetie. *Do* stop doing that while Granny is talking to you.'

Sitting on the low wall near the Doorlings' table and

clocking the scene with interest were two neo Hell's Angels. They had been dragged through a hedge backwards some weeks earlier and hadn't yet had time to get cleaned up, but they appeared to be good-hearted lads and it was to them that Penelope turned for help. Penelope was not only posh, she was pretty, and though she was clearly marked 'Officers Only' she had these two cave men simpering helpfully and looking about for dragons before you could say 'Capitalist's Lackey'. And she could have had them eating out of her hand but it wouldn't have been a very nice experience. She flashed them a charming smile untouched by National Health dentistry and asked them if they'd mind awfully holding Claude as Mummy simply couldn't cope with him. The nearer of the primitives half stood up, baring its fangs. 'Wot,' he said. 'Oh, yeah. Er, 'course. Pleasure, innit,' and took the proffered chain, expertly assessing its combat potential from sheer force of habit. Mummy smiled at him graciously. 'Claude is awfully sweet,' she said, 'and he's not a fighter, you know.' The dog-holder designate was very touched by these democratic advances and responded with all the charm he could muster. 'Oh reely?' he said. 'Wot is 'e then, a sniffer?'

Honey and Gemma were not present on this occasion, not in the pub garden, that is. They were sulking in the car parked under a tree in the car park and from our table we could see Honey lusting after Claude's body and Gemma lusting after scampi and chips, in or out of a basket, or a packet of crisps, Beef and Onion if possible.

We used to take the dogs into any pleasant country pub that would have them and they seemed to realize it was a privilege. They demurely ate any proffered morsels but always refused drinks as they were both under eighteen. There was one particular pub in Hertfordshire that made them very welcome indeed and naturally that was the pub whose hospitality they chose to abuse. The landlord seemed to be very fond of animals. He had an over-sensitive Old English Sheepdog named Umbrage who was rarely seen in the bar as he spent most of his time in the garden brooding over slights and insults, and a loutish and ill natured freeloader of a cat named Pudders. Kind people used to take out titbits to Umbrage and talk to him nicely but it was no use, and Pudders used to lie about on the furniture until he was kicked off it by hard-hearted patrons in search of a seat when he would join Umbrage in the garden and take it out on the birds.

We often used to go to the pub on Saturday lunchtimes in the winter before taking the dogs for a long walk. Had we gone for the walk before going to the pub I doubt if two soggy, mud-smeared wretches dripping smelly water onto the carpets would have been quite so welcome, but of course we never did that and everybody, bar staff and regulars alike, were lulled into what turned out to be a false sense of security by the familiar sight of two nice clean dogs on their absolutely best behaviour sitting under our table and being careful only to salivate on our shoes.

One afternoon Pudders, who had been woken from a cosy dream of having his very own torture chamber instead of having to take captured mice to the garden shed to be interrogated, and been cruelly cuffed by a notorious cat hater who selfishly wanted somewhere to sit, was looking for somebody handy to inflict a sharp pain upon and selected Gemma, who was so bored with behaving herself that she had fallen asleep. We were chatting to a smart middle-aged couple sitting at the next table when Pudders pounced on Gemma's tail and after that things got a bit confused. I can remember a tumult of screams and barks and howls of pain, and gruff and manly voices swearing hard as Pudders went across the room like something horrid off a shovel followed by our table and two raging dogs in furious pursuit. The table went along because the dogs were tethered to it, and strong and angry as they were they found that towing a heavy table about is a considerable handicap when chasing cats. They were snarling over their shoulders at it, and strongly suggesting it should mind its own business, when they barged into our neighbours' table and sent it flying.

I suppose you could calculate, although I certainly couldn't, that a table weighing 56lbs. knocked over by two dogs weighing 4 stones each and travelling at twelve miles an hour would hurl a bar snack x feet into the air, and if you want to check your figures I can tell you that a French bread and butter and an onion soup, a pizza and chips, a Cinzano and lemonade and a pint of bitter got up to about five feet six before loosely coalescing into an unappetizing cloud. It seemed to hang in the atmosphere for a while, before setting off down again at so many feet per second to fall onto anyone not nimble enough to jump out of the way. Our new friends, stunned, maybe, by the suddenness of it all, turned out not to be nimble enough and when the shower was over most of it was over them. I know one's not supposed to laugh at other people's misfortunes, however hilarious they are, and for once I didn't feel like laughing as they looked quite sinister crouching there with pig-swill running down their faces. In fact, they looked like a ghoul and his ghoul friend just come ashore from some bottomless mire and if I'd seen the

'seemed to hang in the atmosphere . . . before setting off again at so many feet per second.'

pair of them in a Hammer House of Horrors movie it would have kept me awake for weeks.

Actually they were not such a pleasant couple as we had first thought. The husband turned out to be humourless and his wife rather hysterical, and although we put their table back and rubbed them down, and proffered drinks and food, they made such a terrible scene that we thought we ought to leave, and never go back, and Gemma didn't help by trying to gobble a sodden piece of cold pizza that was slithering down the woman's leg. The landlord was very reasonable about it all when I rang up to apologize. He said he'd rather enjoyed it as he couldn't stand the couple at any price and suspected the man of being an Income Tax inspector. And somebody told us later that his wife had once said something terribly wounding to Umbrage.

It was funny about Umbrage. I've never thought of Old English Sheepdogs as being very sensitive, and in my experience they certainly don't live up to the soft and cuddly image they have acquired through advertising paint. I've nothing against them as a breed but I wouldn't want to own one, Jane would be constantly at it with a hairbrush and heated rollers, and I've known several with a tendency to be bad tempered. I greeted one cheerily in the park one morning, and chucked it under the chin as I thought we were chums, and the thing absolutely flew at me and frightened me silly before it was dragged off snarling. Its owners swore he was only playing and I suppose that it's possible. Maybe piranha fish have a similar sense of fun. I know I'd hate to fall into a river infested with Old English Sheepdogs, but that's not very likely as they don't seem to be keen on swimming.

Swimming is the only sport that both our dogs enjoy.

That apart, Honey takes after her father, as neither of us have the least interest in ball games, and the only game of any kind that she really enjoys is playing at 'real dogs' which involves sprawling on a sheepskin rug in front of a roaring fire and falling fast asleep.

Gemma is good at games. Not academically very bright perhaps, but good at games, if not over-strong on team spirit. She will play ball games with anybody, invited or not, likes silly games of all kinds and loves imaginative games with fluffy slippers. In this respect she reminds me of the children, not that they chewed up slippers but they liked imaginative games. When they were small we bought them a kiddy car and a tricycle for Christmas and they had a marvellous time playing in the huge boxes that these came in, whilst I, in a desperate bid to inject a little jollity into a family Christmas trundled morosely round the house on the tricycle and slipped a disc while trying to 'pop a wheelie'.

Give Honey a slipper and she takes it off to her small corner and thoughtfully picks it to pieces very precisely with sharp little tugs of the teeth. To Gemma a slipper is all kinds of things, a lurking adversary to be barked at and pounced upon, a fallen bird to be retrieved, or a Zeppelin hovering overhead. Actually 'overstomach' would be a more accurate description as her way of dealing with the Zeppelin menace is to lie on her back and scrabble at them as they drone inexorably in to the attack, with me making noises like a lot of Maybach aero engines and shouting '*Achtung, Achtung.* HMD *Labrador* on the starboard bow, Herr Kapitan.' This can be rather a noisy game and we are not allowed to play it very often as Jane says that the neighbours will begin to talk, especially as the children have grown up and left home. 'Bit of a rumpus in your place this morning, old boy. Everything's all right, I hope?' 'Oh yes, thanks. Just playing Zeppelins with the dogs, you know.'

'Barking Porpoises' is another slipper game that Gemma enjoys. 'Barking' because a slipper game has to have sound effects to be exciting and I suspect that porpoises go in for long mysterious silences. The game is played by folding a fluffy slipper double with the fold between finger and thumb, sole outwards, holding it horizontal, heel uppermost, and opening and shutting it so that the porpoise opens his mouth as he fishtails in to nip at Gemma's legs. The rules are simple. The space between the dogs' bed and our bed is counted as water, and the beds are boats, and porpoises can only attack dogs that are standing in the sea. Jane complains that it is very difficult to read the paper and drink her morning coffee with Gemma leaping about in the scuppers and snarling over the side and a killer porpoise at large in the room. 'Bit of a drama over at your place this morning, old boy. Got a crazed relative locked up in the attic, have we?'

These slipper games, along with two square meals a day, have been very beneficial to Gemma's development as a well-rounded personality but have not been so good for the slippers which have rather a limited life span, and which are never terribly cosy afterwards as they are either soggy or crusty, depending. Honey goes along with Jane and the neighbours and disapproves of boisterous games first thing in the morning, though she will get up and help if Gemma is having a flying lesson. These take place in our bedroom and Gemma sits by the wardrobe at the end of the main runway with her ears flapping up and down and usually gets airborne with excitement after a short run. She hasn't gone solo yet as she can't quite master the ear flapping on her own, and she still has a tendency to bite the instructor, but dog powered flight is in its infancy and waiting for a Mr Wright to come along, but it's still early days.

Another merry game is called 'Taking Gemma's Temperature' because that is what it involves, and we don't play that very often either as Gemma doesn't enjoy it. As you can imagine it isn't done by sticking the instrument under her tongue and taking her pulse at the same time, but by raising the tail and inserting it in a more suitable place, and the first time that Fred committed this outrage poor Gemma was shocked and astonished as she had previously thought of him only as a very dear friend.

Fred had only dropped in on his way home after a hard day's wrestling with small animals and before we offered him drink, from a bottle of twelve-year-old malt that Jane was waving about meaningfully, we asked him if he'd mind having a look at Gemma as she wasn't her cheery self and was moping about looking lack-lustre. Fred said he'd soon get to the bottom of that and his modus operandi was impressively sly. Tearing his eyes from the bottle Jane was holding he scattered a handful of Cheese and Tomato crisps on the carpet and while a poorly Gemma was toying with them he nipped round behind her, singing the Eton Boating Song under his breath, and struck home the thermometer with strength and accuracy. I don't know what he expected Gemma to do. Stand there presumably and play Lady Chatterley to his medicated Mellors. I think he was a bit surprised when she stopped eating and went all rigid – even Gemma can't eat with jaws agape – and then alarmed as she took off as a dervish might in similar circumstances, to go whirling round the living room knocking things over and trying to get her teeth into the intruder, which could have caused complications if a fast moving Fred hadn't brought her down with a crash and pinned her to the parquet just long enough to snatch back his property and get a normal reading.

I've never known just having their temperature taken cure anybody of anything but it was like a tonic to Gemma who perked up immediately, after she'd had a good shake and inspected the affected parts, and Fred said that it just showed what faith she had in his healing powers. Luckily there wasn't a lot of damage. Apart from the half bottle of Scotch that Fred drank, and Gemma's innocence, the only serious casualty was an ashtray that Jane's mother had given us. Made of a bright red glass moulded to a suggestively receptive shape, the family called it the Gynaecologist's Nightmare. It had long since ceased to be a joke and visitors who didn't know about it used to choke on their drinks the moment they caught sight of the thing if any of us were thoughtless enough to mention its name. I can't say I was sorry to see it go. I didn't want to be responsible for anyone's suffering.

Speaking of suffering, I have just been into our bedroom and found both dogs fast asleep on our bed – and this at ten o'clock in the morning. They have only just had their breakfast. Usually they have the decency to fall fast asleep on the furniture downstairs, but I know what it is. Jane is hoovering the sitting room and they hate that. I covered them over and came out quietly. I sometimes wonder if we are not becoming a bit silly about dogs.

All Futura Books are available at your bookshop or newsagent, or can be ordered from the following address:
Futura Books, Cash Sales Department,
P.O. Box 11, Falmouth, Cornwall

Please send cheque or postal order (no currency), and allow 55p for postage and packing for the first book plus 22p for the second book and 14p for each additional book ordered up to a maximum charge of £1.75 in U.K.

Customers in Eire and B.F.P.O. please allow 55p for the first book, 22p for the second book plus 14p per copy for the next 7 books, thereafter 8p per book.

Overseas customers please allow £1.00 for postage and packing for the first book and 25p per copy for each additional book.